The Story of Wyoming Valley

ILLUSTRATED BY THE AUTHOR

S. R. Smith

Author of the *Wyoming Valley in the 19th Century, Daniel North*, &c.

HERITAGE BOOKS
2010

HERITAGE BOOKS

AN IMPRINT OF HERITAGE BOOKS, INC.

Books, CDs, and more—Worldwide

For our listing of thousands of titles see our website
at
www.HeritageBooks.com

A Facsimile Reprint
Published 2010 by
HERITAGE BOOKS, INC.
Publishing Division
100 Railroad Ave. #104
Westminster, Maryland 21157

— Publisher's Notice —
In reprints such as this, it is often not possible to remove blemishes from
the original. We feel the contents of this book warrant its reissue despite
these blemishes and hope you will agree and read it with pleasure.

International Standard Book Numbers
Paperbound: 978-1-58549-750-8
Clothbound: 978-0-7884-8488-9

The Story of Wyoming Valley.

CHAPTER I.

THE HISTORY of Wyoming Valley epitomized in this little story is one of the saddest and most dramatic ever acted. The place in which it was acted is an amphitheatre fashioned by the hand of the Almighty. The arena is a plain, the walls are the blue hills and in the place of silken canopies, the fathomless sky.

Any stranger looking down on this plain from the mountain would feel that in the past men fought with the wild proprietor and with each other to make this secluded portion of the earth their own. We are busy with the fleeting phantom called life, and so fully absorbed that the earth beneath and the sky above has faded as completely as the dreams of our vanished youth. These fields and encircling hills are beautiful, and the short history of the white man since he first came here is more than an idle tale told to occupy an idle hour.

Men and women often have lacked bread for themselves and their children, often shivered with cold and trembled with fear; hardly a home during all the years of struggle but furnished an Indian with a scalp, hardly a mother who was free from the expectation that sooner or later the torch and tomahawk would come and leave only smoking embers and mutilated forms. Thus was a courage born and a manhood developed so splendid as to demand our attention and admiration. The faith of our fathers makes for us a fadeless page from which we learn how to live, for behind the deeds of daring with all the parts of the drama acted, we see plainly something better than the deeds.

A dissolute king brought disaster to honest people by giving the land on which we live to two classes of his subjects. Before any one secured a good title years of blood-shed had to pass. The rival claimants fought as only men will fight when they are fighting for property to which they have a legal right. Then the Indian, with the title that possession gives, spilt blood freely and there is no apology due from him. England was not slow to maintain order in this part of her domain, and there is no apology due from her for doing so. Everybody was right and all of them were wrong. They fought it out and the Yankee conquered the entire combination. When the struggle was ended this valley was his and his heirs'. The state was obliged to give him a valid title to the land and no one has owned an acre of the soil without purchasing it from him.

This continent was divided up among the nations of Europe. The Yankee owned only a strip; he enlarged it until it covered what is now the United States. The entire nation is Yankeeized. Lands across the Atlantic are catching the American spirit, the far east is trying to become inculcated. The great army of strangers from many lands do not materially change anything in our ways of life. The principles on which our national life rests are eternal as the hills; the shore alone on which the tide plays is marked by wreck and debris. The fittist survive, the rest die. There is a reason why the Yankee survived; he alone championed human rights and had the strength to establish them.

Puritan and Yankee are synonymous and when we say New England settler we mean usually the same man. The Puritan means to us a very religious man, one bigoted in the extreme. The truth is he was better than religious, he was better than a church-man simply. All the man was expressed in the principle of religious and civil liberty—he would not wear a yoke. It was a blessed day for humanity when a man was born with courage sufficient to protest and fight against every form of bondage that had oppressed mankind in all the years of the past. His was the first voice that had spoken with real emphasis for freedom. Thank God he made it prevail.

Probably it was necessary and expedient that the church and state should be despotic until humanity were able to think and act without a master. There came a time when men needed a new dispensation, when they had manhood sufficient to demand that no man put a bit in their mouth. The desire for freedom, the strongest desire of man, would assert itself. It did, and every throne since has been insecure.

The men named Puritan protested, not against the religion of the established church and the Roman Catholic Church; they protested against the first because it was a religious monarchy, and the second because it was a religious despotism. They protested against the state because they were through with every form of bondage. It was time that men should shout, "Give me liberty or give me death." Every noble soul the world over responded.

Courage and blood were the coin that purchased the pearl so desirable. England was smeared with blood, royalty was trodden under foot, Cromwell fought and Milton wrote.

Neither England nor the Puritans discovered America. Spain alone had a claim to the continent. A claim is not enough in this world, it is necessary that the claim be defended, and a stronger power than Spain was needed to resist the long arm and the grasping hand of England. It may be true that only English men could have successfully unpinned the English yoke.

We call our fathers rebels, bigots, and heretics. Read the Declaration of Independence and the Constitution of the United States to be convinced that they were splendid infidels. Every paragraph is a cutting loose from creeds of all kinds and of oppression of every kind. These documents declare for freedom for the whole people. The men who formed and established this government were not sectarians. Thomas Jefferson, James Hamilton, George

Washington, Thomas Paine—in fact nearly all of them like Lincoln trusted in God and their own power without consulting any creed or asking the sanction of any denomination. Emerson was a deeply pious man. In his attitude towards the teaching and the authority of the church he was a typical Puritan. It is easy reading to spell out the reason why this government endures and resists; why it gathers under its protection men of all nationalities and religious beliefs.

The colonists from England that settled in the south were not Puritans. They were English aristocrats, they established an aristocracy. We learned when they tried to dissever this nation that they were not patriots. No wonder that England aided them and rejoiced in the prospect that the Yankee was to be conquered and stripped of his power. The fool and the knave at home and abroad have learned the folly of striking and attacking the guardians of our rights and contending against the principles this government embodies.

There never lived a man more interesting or more worthy of our admiration than the Puritan. Every inhabitant of this valley, be he Catholic or Protestant, is indebted to him for civil and religious liberty and to some extent for the prosperity he enjoys. Any one who reads the history of this valley will marvel at and admire the perseverance of the saints and recognize the hand of God in our history.

The thread of red that is woven in our history is blended in the background giving a sinister effect to the picture as well as an unmistakable attractiveness that awakens within us a feeling akin to admiration. The Indian worshiped the moon and threw tobacco in the fire for incense. We are a little shocked at the way he was treated and perfectly satisfied with the result.

The Moravian missionaries were the first white men to come here. The settlers that came after them were not missionaries to the Indians in any sense. They built more distilleries than churches, they gave the savage the bottle and not the Bible.

To a limited extent we are interested in the Indian. The fragrant memories of childhood that linger in the recesses of our minds have a wild charm due to the tales told us of the spectacular red man by the royal entertainers of our youth. We can recall the Indian as we then beheld him in our vision. We were told how wild and wicked he was but we thought differently and the opinion of those days still dominates us. Consequently when we read how black he was we persist in leaving him red with the addition of war paint and his picturesque environment. We are not complimentary and rarely just when we discuss a heathen. The Indian probably rated the white man more astutely than he was rated, at least, it is evident, that the red man knew on which side to stand during the war between the English and the French and later how to stand by the enemy of the settlers. He sold the land when he could no longer hold it and for most of it received as much as it was worth at that time. The leaders could hold their own in council with all the talent and culture arrayed against them. They fully realized the size of the white man's foot and the strength of his arm.

The Indian problem is about disposed of. Civilization had no mission for him, or designed to have, that would benefit him. It is not proven by any means that he could not have made a consistent Christian and a reputable citizen. The Five Nations or the Six Nations as they became later on, carried the science of government to a point that awakens our admiration. This federation of nations was as unique and complete in its way as any we have read of in the history of the world. Their form of government was despotic with supreme power centered in a council made up of representatives of the tribes that formed the confederation. Tioga Point, near what is now Athens, was the headquarters of the Indians in this section. Here all the renegades, as well as the Tories of the region adjoining, congregated. Here they built towns and planned their raids upon the whites. Here Queen Esther had her village and from this point came the force that effectually effaced the Yankee from the valley for a time.

A large number of the families of this locality removed to different points between here and the state line and in many ways our history reaches out to the Chemung River and beyond, as well as down the river to Sunbury where Fort Augusta was erected and served both as a prison and a defence.

The Indians of the valley were mostly Delawares, completely under the rule of the Six Nations. There were not many Indians in the valley after the settlers came and it was mainly after the massacre that they were a real menace to the people. Without warning they would sweep in and massacre a family, probably take one or more of the children with them and vanish, not often occupying more than a few minutes to complete their work. It was rarely that a pursuit proved successful. In the state there were over three hundred children returned from captivity after peace was declared. Some wished to remain with the captors. A sad feature of their return was that in many cases no relatives could be found to claim them. Orphans and widows were seeking protection and help in every direction. Notwithstanding the impoverished condition of the people most of the time and the constant plundering and destruction of crops, the helpless found bread and shelter, even to the sharing of the last meal. And yet these people would come back every time they were driven out and hold on to their beautiful domain with the patience of death. These strenuous times make our strenuous lives appear only child's play, and our poverty plenty and to spare.

CHAPTER II.

UR VALLEY, as we behold it, is beautiful and picturesque; as the first band of settlers beheld it, it was wild and sublime. Few of us have looked over a valley like ours covered with primeval forest. The picture staggers the most powerful imagination. Of the life the Indians lived where we have found a place of abode and the splendor and beauty of their haunts under the deep shade of the yellow pine, the maple, oak and button-wood, we have no conception.

The fame of this inviting spot had spread all over the colonies and was being taken across the sea by every vessel. The New Englander wanted to turn his back upon the stony soil and the chilling winds that swept over the hills from the sea, and make himself a home between these blue hills where God had performed His master stroke, where the soil was waiting to bring forth abundantly and nature was lavish with her gifts.

At Hartford, Connecticut, The Susquehanna Company was formed in the year 1754. They purchased land along the Susquehanna of the Six Nations for two thousand pounds. The territory is described as being over one hundred and twenty miles in length and sixty in breadth. They had a charter granted by King George the Second, dated April 23, 1662, granting them that portion of his domain lying between the 41st and 42nd degrees of latitude and extending across what they supposed was a narrow continent.

The proprietors of Pennsylvania had also a charter for the same territory granted by the same sovereign, given to William Penn in 1681. These claimants prepared to resist the claims of the Yankee, a thing which they did for over forty years.

We now come to the original shove; all the rest will follow. In the Nutmeg State a number of families were ready to stake life and fortune on a bold venture. The body of men forming what is known as the Susquehanna Company wisely commissioned some they thought competent to go and view the promised land. These agents viewed the land and tried to conciliate the Indians in advance to the invasion of their choice hunting ground. These men returned and reported favorably. In the interval before the little company reached the valley the state claimants, having learned what was taking place, hastened to send troops to the valley assume military occupation.

The story of the first attempt to settle the valley by the people from Connecticut is a fitting prelude to what took place afterwards. These adventurers doubtlessly shouted with joy as they beheld this garden in the wilderness for the first time and considered themselves fortune's favorites. They were not favorites,—quite the reverse. They were to be the first victims of the host that afterwards would suffer and die in securing a permanent home on these lowlands between these hills.

It was not necessary for them to clear land, for on the flats on the east side they found soil ready for the plow.

They built log houses, and planted crops. Their friends in the east heard only glowing reports from them until a message came that the entire settlement had been wiped out by the Indians, some of the settlers having escaped to tell their friends of the sad tragedy.

The experiences of some of the men who escaped massacre would please a lover of stories of adventures. One man crawled into a hollow log to hide from the Indians that were following him. An Indian came and sat on the log. Finally he looked in the end and seeing a cobweb stretched across the opening he was certain that his intended victim was not there. This cobweb story has a flavor of age about it; that nevertheless does not make it impossible for history to repeat itself.

The people in the east considered they had a valid title to the land that a king had deeded to them and ornamented with his great seal. They were eager to migrate to the beautiful valley on the Susquehanna of which they had heard so many glowing accounts. They proposed to come prepared to defend themselves and make a permanent settlement.

The war between the French and English had just closed, the French having ceded the northern portion of the continent to the English. The Indians, now that they were not helping foreigners to fight each other, began fierce warfare against the whites. The West Branch was settled and the Indians plundered, burned and murdered without mercy along this tributary of our river as well as in other sections of the states.

The English and Germans had settled along the Delaware and were the other owners of the coveted territory. When they learned of the preparations going on in the east to attempt settlement here a second time they leased this valley to three men, Ogden, Stewart, and Jennings, for seven years, divided it into two manors, and military occupation was declared.

The Susquehanna Company divided this section into five townships, five miles square, and then subdivided a portion of it into forty shares as a free will offering to the forty pioneers. Two hundred pounds were given them to purchase farm implements with which to cultivate the land. The forty came here in February, 1769, and two hundred followed the next spring.

To round out our story we will consider the state of affairs in the colonies. The second settlement of the valley was six years before Paul Revere took his famous ride and the first shot of the Revolution was fired. One of the worst sovereigns of modern times, sat on the English throne, and parliament which twelve years before, had begun to impose taxation without representation, proposed, when the war between France and England closed in 1762, to pay the enormous war debt by imposing additional tax upon the colonies. The Declaration of Independence that Patrick Henry had voiced was stirring men's hearts. As they had never seen a king, were dissenters in religion and republicans in politics, for six generations had governed themselves, had been shown by the French and Indian war that they could defend themselves, when the Stamp Act of 1765 was passed the flaming fire of independence blazed fierce. Added to this was the inherited character of the colonist and we might add the knowledge that when the French king signed the treaty with England after the war and ceded Canada to their conquerors, it was to make it possible for the creation of a republic in the west that would trample the standard of St. George in the dust. The imperative necessity to secure subsistence as well as the Englishman's desire for property and the innate desire, common to all men for liberty, prompted the breaking away from the monarchial government under which for generations their ancestors had lived where the monarch seldom regarded the rights and the welfare of his subjects with anything less than contempt. All these things combined, prompted the strong men of the colonies to come to this valley, and they at first established a democracy as untrammeled by outside authority as that enjoyed by the American savage. These men had iron in their souls and muscles of steel; they had not outgrown the superstition of the past. They believed in witches as their progenitors had believed the world to be flat. It is no slander to say they were chiefly concerned and occupied in looking after their own interests and that they enjoyed strife. Before they left New England they drew up laws to govern them and made the town meeting the center of authority.

When they reached the valley Ogden, Stewart and Jennings, the lessees, occupied the land under military protection of the state. They had erected forts and block-houses and were trying to make settlements in the valley. They lived mostly in the forts they had erected and compelled the New Englanders to fight constantly to protect themselves.

The five townships allotted to the settlers were surveyed, and Kingston township, the first that was occupied was allotted to the favored forty. Most of the lowlands were free from trees and covered with rank grass. The soil was very rich, consequently large crops could be raised with little labor. With the river full of shad, in their season, and other fish in great abundance wild meat always within reach, they were secure from want. The winter having passed they were ready to put in their crops.

They built Fort Durkee near Fish Eddy, the fort at Mill Creek, built by the first settlers, being too remote, as they were cultivating the flats below the present site of Wilkes-Barre. By May they numbered 280 able-bodied men. The eyes of the new-comers were opened to the beauty and wealth of their possessions.

The state authorities sent a force to the valley, but after they had beheld the means of defence and the number of the enemy they were sent to wage war against, they returned to Easton. There was a small force in the Pennamite forts, and the three Pennsylvania proprietors, Ogden, Stewart and Jennings were absent, Jennings was a civil magistrate. The governor sent a company from Philadelphia to drive the Yankees out. This company encamped at Fort Durkee, but not daring to make an assault they removed to a safe place and awaited reinforcements. This

Before the White Man came.

was in June. In September, the prince of trouble makers, Ogden, with Sheriff Jennings, came with three hundred men. They arrested the leader of the settlers, Captain Durkee, and took him in irons to Philadelphia. With so large a force against them, their leader a captive, and the terrifying boom of a small cannon ringing in their ears, the besieged men surrendered. All were ordered out of the country except the seventeen men to look after the crops, these were ordered out later. With their dream shattered and their prospects blighted the bold pioneers turned their faces to the east. Then the brave and bold Lazarus Stewart appeared on the scene. He captured that awful cannon. The victorious Ogden retired to Fort Ogden only to surrender and defeat. The farmers burned the fort and confiscated all the enemey's property to make good the loss they had sustained when they were driven out.

The men who had left the valley against their will came back full of fight. They were in possession and before their blood had come to cool off, the governor, a great grandson of the splendid American and friend and favorite of royalty, William Penn, but who lacked all the glorious perogatives of his great grandfather, called upon General Gage, commander of the Continental troops, to drive the awful Yankees back to the Nutmeg State. The General promptly replied that it would be highly improper for the King's troops to interfere in a matter of property between the people.

Peace reigned again, a prosperous summer followed, the Forty Fort was builded. Then Ogden came back by an unguarded route, seized the men in the field unarmed at their work. This was in September. Ogden captured fort Durkee and its defenders, sent Captain Zebulon Butler and Spalding, with other leaders, to Philadelphia as prisoners. The men were taken to Easton.

The Pennamites supposed they were through with the Yankee. Consequently they left only a handful of soldiers to defend the forts. Lazarus Stewart was on the war trail. In December he swept down on the forts and the garrison fled, most of them protected only by the one garment they had on when Stewart's men disturbed their dreams.

In 1770, Ogden came in the dead of winter with one hundred men. He built a fort sixty rods from Fort Durkee and called it Wyoming. Then he demanded the surrender of the enemy. In the attack on Fort Durkee, Ogden's brother was killed, and Ogden retired. Stewart knowing how highly he was prized by the state authorities retired in the night to the mountain, leaving a few men in the fort. These Ogden sent to Easton as prisoners, after which he strengthened his position and wondered doubtless where that awful Stewart was. A child never feared the dark or a culprit the lash as Stewart was feared, and the state authorities at this time doubled the reward they had offered for his arrest. They would wipe the settlers nearly out of existence and then this brave and bold cavalier would ap-pear with the Paxton boys, and Ogden and his followers would scatter.

The next time the curtain rises on the stage we see Capt. Zebulon Butler, whom we supposed a prisoner of war in

Philadelphia, and Lazarus Stewart with one hundred and fifty men cooping Ogden up in Fort Wyoming on the river bank. Butler and Stewart built a fort a short distance below Fort Wyoming. To-day two granite blocks, properly inscribed, rest on the river bank to point out where they were. Then some fortifications were erected across the river and something of the kind on the Redout where the new court house stands. That terrible cannon was mounted upon this elevation and probably made the shad in the river jump out of their bed. Ogden wanted help and he wanted it very bad, so he performed an act that is the only clever thing recorded in his career. He rolled up his clothes, placed his hat on them, tied a cord to the bundle, and with this he floated down stream a short distance keeping his nose out of the water and hanging on to the end of the string. As he passed the sentinels they riddled his hat with bullets. Thus he escaped, going on foot to Philadelphia. Later on he is back again with reinforcement. These Butler ambushes. Ogden goes back over his tracks, and the men are allowed to find refuge in the fort of their friends to help eat up the food of the besieged who are soon obliged to capitulate.

Thus ends the first Pennamite war which lasted three years and brings us now to September, 1771.

CHAPTER III.

WE HAVE come to the days that are the most beautiful in our history when peace and prosperity were enjoyed. The men built homes and removed their families from the east. Every man was the dictator of his own acts and had no master except his own will. A Utopian condition of human existence was realized that was better than Plato's dream. Block houses were erected on both sides of the river, and territory surveyed and assigned to the settlers. People began to flock here from every direction. They were so well occupied that they had no time to think of a regular form of government, settled their disputes by a town committee. They had order without law or a constable. There was, strange to say, religious tolerance more than we find among them at an earlier day. Ferries were erected, mills and distilleries built and roads made. As soon as the people had provided for their maintenance they brought teachers and preachers here and provided for the support of the churches and the school. By 1773, by the increase of the population and conflicting interests it became necessary to have a form of government. To meet this need the Susquehanna Company adopted a code of laws and means to enforce them.

At this time the Connecticut people tried to open negotiations with the Pennsylvania claimants to settle the dispute over the territory. These offers were spurned.

It 1774 all the territory from the Delaware to fifteen miles beyond the Susquehanna was erected in a town, called

Westmoreland, and attached to Litchfield county. This was seventy miles square and was divided into townships, then into lots that were sold or assigned to the settlers by drawing lots. The governor of the state forbade the settlers settling on the land and claimed the territory. The population at this time was about 3,000. The people met and elected officers, their government being under the protection of the colonists, while they waited the pleasure of the crown.. Their form of government was an independent democracy. Up to this time every man was a soldier, paid or unpaid, and worked with a gun swung over his back.

Let us imagine a walk through the valley on a pleasant day at the time of which we are writing. The people we would meet would be variously clad, in keeping with a period emerging from the most primitive state. Yet some things would not be so strange to us. We would see the doe-skin dandy and the home-spun dude, the artful maiden anxious to make an impression, and the lady of fashion as artificial proportionately as we have to-day. The typical hunter's dress would be seen and evidences of military life and customs.

The whipping post and the stocks would be there while the one-story log cabin would be the most conspicuous order of architecture to be seen. We would perceive that young Matthias Hollenback had opened a store, the first and probably the only merchant. The name of nearly all the persons you meet would be familiar notwithstanding the fact that they lived over four generations ago. There will be no streets worthy of the name and no side-walks. From any part of the town you could look north, south and east right into the wildest woods you ever saw and see the river by looking towards the flats. The most interesting objects seen will be the forts. We will go down to what is now the river common, between South and Ross streets, where we will find a fort the most interesting in the valley, and as we have just read of some events that transpired there we are aware that it is Fort Durkee. It was built of hewn logs, is about half-acre in extent and is surrounded by ramparts and intrenchments. Near it we find some twenty houses with loop-holes. Later on it became the headquarters for General Sullivan, when he came here after the Revolution to drive out the Indians. We will take a look at Fort Wyoming, a little more than a rifle-shot away, built by Ogden to aid him in fighting the Yankee. We will go up to Mill Creek where the people have built a mill to grind their grain. Here we will find a fort named after the creek. Within we will see huts that the settlers lived in most of the time during the three bloody years just passed. At the Redout we will find a fortification mounted with the famous cannon that Ogden frightened the inhabitants with a few years before. These forts are interesting yet we remember they never were atacked by the Indians or were the scene of much bloodshed. Forty Fort interests us more for it is larger, incloses an acre of ground, and is made of two thicknesses of logs twelve feet above ground, with a watch-tower at each corner. Inside we find barracks and huts built along the wall so that the soldiers could stand on the roofs to fire at the enemy. We go down through a sunken passage to the edge of the river where there is a spring. By going up to what is now Sturmersville we see Wintermute fort. We do not find friends for they are mostly Tories. We go to the Jenkin's fort, nearly a mile above on the river bank. By ferrying across the river we look at Fort Pittston, composed of thirty-five log houses, built in a triangle and connected at the upper story. From this fort the people who had gathered there during the invasion of the Indians, British and Tories, witnessed the battle and the awful scene in the evening when Queen Esther wrote her name blood red in history. This fort surrendered the day after and, as at the other forts, the Indians appropriated everything they wanted. The Indians smeared black paint on their prisoners' faces to protect them from harm. We will go back down the valley. We can follow an Indian trail or take a canoe.

We want to see the public buildings of Wilkes-Barre. We find the jail and all the municipal buildings in a fort standing on what is now Public Square. This fort is called Wilkes-Barre. Here once stood an Indian village called Wyoming. There is a block-house that is situated down towards Nanticoke. When we say it is Lazarus Stewart's property and is near his home it is certain that any one who loves a hero would walk the distance to visit this land buccaneer. If we had the making of monuments, and the erecting of memorials, this favorite of ours would have one worthy of the man and the deeds he performed. He fell in the battle of Wyoming. His compatriots, Zebulon Butler and Colonel Durkee, the hard fighter, proved impervious to bullets and the hemp noose designed for them by their enemies, and died peacefully in their beds long after the war dogs and the wolves had ceased to howl in the valley. On our way down we will see where the cabin stood that the Pennamites built for the notable Delaware chief Tedeuscung. This friend of the white people awakened the jealousy of the Six Nations, who sent a party here to put him out of the way, an end they accomplished by burning him in his cabin in the night. Some claim that he was sleeping off the effects of liquor which the visitors had given him while his guests, and pretending to be his friends.

There are many old families living here and there in this end of the valley. It is apparent that the population of the country is being provided for as most families have from ten to fifteen children and often more. At this time the log school house and the teacher that boards around has not become one of the institutions of the valley to any extent. It was not expensive to raise a family. As bears and deer would come poking about within rifle range from the cabin door to investigate their neighbors it was easy to keep a barrel of wild meat on hand and fresh meat on their table all the year round. There were no game laws and the men were good marksmen. Down in this neighborhood that terror of the Indians, the famous Inman family lived. We wonder what became of the old rifle that old Inman talleyed by a notch every Indian he shot.

We go down to the gorge in the mountain where the river leaves the valley. Here the Nanticokes reared their teppe while up the river on the other side the Shamokins had a village. It was to these Indians that Count Zinzendorf preached. This missionary is associated in our minds with the legend, or snake story in which history pictures him reading his Bible in his tent by a fire. Two red faces and the gleam of a knife are seen in the opening in the tent. The Indians observe a snake, evidently thawed out by the fire, crawling over the count's garment as it made its way out. The story may be only a story yet it reveals the danger this saint was exposed to in his work. The Indians thought the preacher was one clothed with divine power, he having a poisonous reptile for his companion. The superstition of these would-be murderers served a better purpose than usual, as the proposed tragedy did not take place.

We follow along a well-worn Indian trail over which the Senecas, Cayugas and Oneidas as well as other tribes have traveled, for the great Indian highway between the north and south was through this valley. There is no doubt that Cornplanter, Red Jacket, Brant (the Mohawk chief, who was a British officer in epulets and an educated man), and other noted chiefs passed this way. Away back in 1739 Conrad Weiser, the noted interpreter who spread the fame of the valley far and wide, doubtless traveled this road.

Here in this end of the valley in 1775 occurred a conflict that gives us considerable satisfaction, although it was designed to disturb the peace and prosperity that reigned. Colonel Plunket came up the river with a force of seven hundred men. Butler and Stewart went to Nanticoke to receive him. Stewart took the west side and Butler the east, where he erected breast works. The defending force numbered only two hundred and fifty men. Butler, out of the

kindness of his heart, fired a blank volley. Then Plunket
went over to Stewart's side of the river. Stewart, with
charasteric unkindness to a foe, fired bullets. The balls
came so rapid and straight that Plunket changed his mind,
and decided that Northumberland was a safer place than
Nanticoke.

Wherever we go it is evident the people are on the verge
of war with the mother country. When the Declaration of
Independence was declared in 1776, the whole section was
as wildly aflame as any part of the country.

It is interesting to come on a cabin in the woods for the
family as well as the dogs give you a boisterous welcome.
Public opinion was not shaped by the press and a newspaper
like we read would have created more of a sensation than a
visit from the king. The tongue was mightier than the
pen, and every traveler was expected to stop, tell the family
the news from the outside world, be treated to all the
whiskey he wanted and depart with the knowledge that he
had called upon those who were very glad to see him. A
family would have felt humiliated to the last degree if they
were caught without liquor in the house. These people
loved to talk, they loved to gossip as well as we do. They
would get together and tell more interesting things than we
read in the paper. Every man bragged about himself and
blowed about the villainy of the despised foe. The awful stories the women would tell about witches, spooks,
warnings and the omens of their dreams were believed. The
children would listen to them as eagerly as to the words of

the Bible. They would jump at any unusual sound and gape in wonder. The young men did not know how to tie a four-in-hand, yet it must be born in mind they knew how to court a girl and marry her without delay.

The men wearing a queue and knee breeches causes us to realize how differently we dress as well as that our style of apparel can not compare with theirs in picturesqueness. The moccasin did not have high heels, neither did it warn the wild animals of the approach of the hunter, nor was it liable to produce corns. We may as well envy as pity the pioneer. They had great times, the food they ate as we consider their bill of fare, makes us wish we could make them a visit. They had plenty of the best meat a man ever ate. Corn cake, which is not bad eating, roast beans, and the great fruit of our forefathers, the pumpkin, wild grapes and wild berries as well as cider and nuts. Of course we prefer steam heat yet the great open fire place where the family and neighborly neighbors, told better stories than we hear and as true, blazed hospitably. They were the heroes of all the yarns they spun. The men still wore their hair long. It was not until Burgoyne, with his last ship load of British soldiers left Philadelphia for home, that the queue went the way of other things that were discarded at this time. They had the real Yankee drawl, their talk sounding as queer as their writing reads. Their food and their fun we can comprehend, but how they could set at table with a few pewter platters and iron knives and forks, get along without wooden floors and nothing better than stools and benches to sit on, is more than we can understand. These people were mostly aristocrats with the best manners and breeding. The old men could bow to a lady elaborately, and the wives and daughters could courtsey to perfection. The attempt to imitate the manners of royalty was evident in all their social life. Their loud hearty laughter made it apparent that nature was the teacher that guided them to a very great extent. It should be born in mind how, in their birth and breeding, as well as in contact with life, that they were not common or inferior—quite the reverse. No men had better blood in their veins or more creditible history. They were the flower of New England and the full bloom of the greatest people in the world. It is safe to say they were not provincial to any extent or so cut off from the world as to confine their interest and outlook to their surroundings.

As we travel around among them, even in our imagination it is not easy to forget how soon these happy homes are to be only a memory, the people murdered, their habitations destroyed, and themselves driven back east stripped of everything, even of the necessities of life.

We say "Milly me," thankful our fate is more fortunate. We do not forget how many men of character and brains, and lovely women have hated, fought, suffered, loved and died between these mountains. How many admirable traits these transplanted and transformed Puritans possessed. We are proud of our history as well as of our progenitors. Now we will devote our attention to the most dramatic part of the history of Wyoming Valley.

CHAPTER IV.

A NEW NATION is about to be born, a new flag is to spread out its beautiful folds over the freest nation in the history of the world; one to become the greatest. England is preparing for war and the colonies have raised the cry, "Liberty or death." The people are divided, many determined to be loyal to the crown and to cast their fortune with the strongest force. The Indian, to strike his dangerous enemy who was crowding him out of his old haunts, was ready to spill blood and apply the torch if he was paid and protected. The people in the valley were ready to do their share of fighting against the three powerful opponents to be pitted against them.

The claim of an exercise of arbitrary government by Great Britian was the principal cause of the revolution, for since 1748, when England began to enforce her claim the revolution had been brewing. France had constantly excited a spirit of resistance in the colonies. These men had not forgotten the circumstances under which their ancesters had left their homes. The growth of the spirit of independence had led them to believe that complete separation from England was desirable and possible. The thick-headed and narrow George the Third, who sat on the throne for sixty years, and his bigoted and incompetent ministers, widened the breach that finally became so wide that nothing could hold the two countries together. After the Stamp Act was passed in 1765, the Sons of Liberty was organized.

The colonist refused to purchase English goods. The Boston massacre took place, and in 1773 the Boston tea party was held. In 1774 the second colonial congress met in Philadelphia and the result was that General Gage was sent across the sea with a fleet and ten thousand soldiers, Paul Revere and his famous ride and the War of the Revolution was on. George Washington was appointed commander-in-chief of the Federal troops, numbering fourteen thousand five hundred volunteers. On July the fourth, at two o'clock in the afternoon, 1776, the Declaration of Independence was adopted, the King's Arms was torn down and burned in the streets of Philadelphia.

The dark war cloud threw its shadow across these hills and over this plain. It reached even to the most solitary home, causing the most intense excitement and awakening the spirit of patriotism in every heart. Men gathered together to discuss the news and to pick up every scrap of information from the coast. There were few men in the valley who were inexperienced in the trade of war or wished to be away from the scene of conflict. After the first blow was struck it was necessary that the war must be fought to the end. Trouble rarely comes alone. At this time it appears as if all hades was let loose upon this isolated spot unprotected by outside selp. Consequently the Connecticut authorities acted a contemptible part. The old enemy over the southern mountain sent Plunket with an army that outnumbered the able-bodied men in the valley, and the savages at Tioga Point became a menace. It is evident that every man was needed at home, as there was trouble, and serious trouble looming up in every direction. That reptile of the revolution, the Tory, was spawned—the worst and last pestilence to be contended with.

It is understood the Tories were settlers who came here from New York, mostly settling at the upper end of the valley, probably compelled to, do so. It is supposed that they persuaded John Butler to come here and strike the settlement.

The offence that Connecticut committed against the people was to forbid emigration here at the time of the greatest need.

At this time, 1776, orders were given to form the 24th regiment of Connecticut militia in Westmoreland. During this year, the people invited the Indians to come here and hold a council. Captain John spoke for the Indians and Butler for the whites. The Indians proposed that they come here and live with their white brother in peace. That the savages wanted to put themselves in position to murder the inhabitants was understood.

It became absolutely necessary that the people have protection, and Congress stationed two companies here. These companies were raised here, and were stationed one on the west and the other on the east side of the river. Among those who enlisted a squad of men was Matthias Hollenback. Before the year was out Howe had driven Washington out of New York into New Jersey. Washington was obliged to send for the Westmorland companies, presumably for only a short time. The people strengthened their forts and sent scouts up the river to watch the Indians, under the charge of Lieut. John Jenkins, a surveyor and the moderator of the great town meeting held previous to this. He was captured by the Indians. The story of his release by an Indian he contracted a friendship with is interesting. During this period the people on the east and west side contended to see if the public buildings for the county should be located in Kingston or Wilkes-Barre. The people on the east side won.

Vagabond Indians came prowling through the valley, the squaws begging. These were supposed to be spies. A man was shot up the river. All indications pointed to an invasion from the north. The women petitioned and prayed for the return of their natural protectors all in vain, for the Continental army was in awful straits. These were the darkest days and the most trying days in our history. No one could see anything ahead except a final catastrophe, when the wave beaten raft on which the seekers after liberty were clinging would be torn apart, leaving the victims to the mercy of what they feared as much as death itself. From this distance it is evident how securely they were riding a treacherous tide to the realization of more than the surmounting of the difficulties that confronted them. Faith in God was the rock on which the Puritan and his descendants stood. This enduring faith was where the arm of flesh raised against them failed and proved ineffectual.

The battle and massacre of Wyoming stands out in our nation's history as one of the most important and unique

The Battle and Massacre of Wyoming.

events on record. The reason it has gained so much fame and luster is principally because the Yankee was astute enough to make it advertise to the world the awful results that came from the employment of savages to murder and burn white people and practice their terrible methods of warfare. The opportunity was not unimproved. It could not have been used better by the expert advertisers of the present. No similar attempt has met with such success. All through the history of this country the press has served the contestants as effectually as the armies in the field, and often more so. If we had the accounts that were written by these slick Yankees, and first published in Poughkeepsie, and read them, we might fully comprehend how clever the writers were. The awful story of our wrongs were read all over the civilized world with pity and horror. The English people hung their heads in shame. Parliament refused to appropriate money to continue the war. This fact places the little fight up above Wyoming as one of the most important events of the War of the Revolution.

The Indian struck the individual and his battle-field was the settlers' cabin. He was not a soldier, and that is why his name is held as a synonym of all that is hateful to civilized man. The crimes he committed here were no worse than what he was guilty of all over the colonies. The story that made such a sensation had an appropriate background that made the picture complete.

Looking over the names of the officers who commanded the men at Wyoming we conclude they did not lack experience or ability. In fact the force was well officered.

Zebulon Butler and Lazarus Stewart were experienced men. They had fought in the war that had just closed and Butler was here on furlow from the storm center of the war that was being waged for independence. Durkee and Ransom, who reached the valley just in time to go into the fight had also come here from the seat of war. Lieut. Col. George Dorrance, Colonel Denison, and Major Garret, were able officers. It must not be inferred that all the able-bodied men were off to war. Nearly every one of the old families of the valley was represented by one or more members. By looking over the list of the men that were slain or that escaped, this fact becomes apparent.

When it became known that Col. John Butler was up near the state line preparing to make a descent upon the settlers, companies were formed and the raw recruits drilled. Every preparation was made and the people warned to flee to the forts for protection. The enemy came down the river to Bowman's Creek, then across the mountain to Fort Wintermute. Here were the Jenkins, Harding, and Gardner families. On June 30th the Harding massacre occurred. Eight men not aware of the presence of the enemy, had gone to Exeter to work on their land. The Indians found and attacked them. Wallace, Gardner and Car were taken prisoners, two of the Hardings were killed and two of the Hadsells. John Harding, a boy, hid in the water under the bushes and escaped. Word of this tragedy came to the valley on the first of July. Colonel Butler sent Lieut. Col. Dorance and Colonel Denison with their companies up to Exeter. They found two Indians on guard, whom they shot. Colonel Butler buried the men at Fort Jenkins, which is now West Pittston. After Colonel Butler had returned to Forty Fort the invaders took possession of Fort Wintermute. At this fort we have the record of one man, David Ingersoll, who tried, unassisted, to fight the foe. The Tories captured and bound him. In the evening John Butler sent a force up to fort Jenkins to capture it. There were seventeen old men to defend it. After four were killed and three captured the rest surrendered.

On the morning of the second, John Butler sent his prisoner, Gardner, with an escort to Forty Fort, to demand that the fort and camp be surrendered. These demands were refused. Friday, the third, the day of the fight, Gardner with another white man and an Indian were again sent. The settlers suspected the Indian and the white man who escorted Gardner came to ascertain the strength of the fortification and the number of the defenders.

It is the blood-red letter day of our history. The famous cannon is booming at Fort Wilkes-Barre to warn the settlers of the impending storm. There was a strange sight witnessed that morning and the previous. Little and big groups were hurrying from their homes hidden in the nooks and corners, with bundles of provision and little else, to the forts. Some probably brought a cow to supply the children with milk, with now and then a horse to bear the aged and sick. We refuse to let our thoughts dwell on the scenes that occurred as each family left all they possessed. The unwritten history of the past was enacted, and we care not to reproduce it. All the families did not come, many of them lived in the lower end and off along the foot of the mountains. After the surrender of the fort, these families went down the river in boats. Some of them may have remained, or taken to the woods. At all the places of defence a few old men and boys remained. Captain Blanchard was at the fort at Pittston with a small company. Spaulding who was coming with help from the seat of war was forty miles away.

We wish we had a good picture of the council that Colonel Butler held, the morning of the third, with his officers. By invitation he had assumed command. There were several army officers at this council and in the fight that served as privates. Butler and Stewart appear to have had the most authority. Butler counciled staying in the fort and Stewart vigorously insisted going to meet the enemy. Denison and Dorrance advised waiting, hoping Spaulding would come. Stewart had the majority with him, while the most level-headed were with Butler; but the latter, against his better judgment consented to lead the men out. As we can not tell what the outcome would have been if they had remained in the fort, we cannot pass judgment on the decision.

There were six irregular companies in the fort. These were from Hanover, Plymouth, Wilkes-Barre and Kingston, mostly raw recruits. There were 230 men enrolled, the rest being civil magistrates, old men, boys, and other volunteers. This force marched out to engage the enemy five miles away, late in the afternoon. Half an hour after they departed, Captains Durkee and Pierce came riding up to the fort, having left Spaulding in the swamp, when they learned that the men were on their way to meet the enemy. They hurried to join them and were killed.

As the little army approached Wyoming they saw the flames ascending from Fort Wintermute. Colonel Butler sent four of his officers ahead to select a spot and mark off the ground on which to form the order of battle. The spot selected was on the upper flat, the steep bank on the right and the swamp on the left. We infer that the place was more or less open. The beautiful afternoon sunshine flooded the place, the repose of a summer's day making the scene as peaceful and sweet as a child's sleep. The men were formed in battle lines, the companies of Gore and Hewitt on the right. Colonel Butler, Colonel Bidlack and Major Garret supported this wing. Colonel Denison, supported by Lieut, Col. George Dorrance, commanded the left wing with Captain Whittsley on the extreme left. Butler made a brief address. He said: "Men, yonder is the enemy. The fate of the Hardings tell us what we may expect if we are defeated. We came out to fight, not only for liberty, but for life itself, and what is dearer, to preserve our homes from conflagration and our women and children from the tomahawk. Stand firm the first shock and the Indians will give way. Every man to his duty." Colonel Butler ordered his columns to display. They marched up to the right. The left of the enemy's forces rested on Fort Wintermute, which was in flames.

Col. Zebulon Butler ordered his men to fire and then take a step ahead. Then the inspiring and blood-stirring report of guns rang out all along the line. Blood began to flow and the cold hand of death began to claim its victims. A continuous stream of lead was poured into the columns of men before them. They could not face the fire and began to fall back. Behind the steep bank on the right, between the upper and lower flats, a party of Indians were pouring into our exposed men a destructive fire. The indians on the left began firing. The fight grew fierce, the indians started their fearful yell which was answered by the Indians on the other side. This appeared to be a signal for a rush. The fight had continued for a half-hour. From out of the swamp the Indians came with a yell. On they came like fiends, rushed into the left wing of their foes and cut them off. Every soldier knew that the battle had ended and a hand to hand struggle for life was before them. An attempt of Denison to turn the left wing to face the red men in the rear completely failed. The primitive, one-man fight, was on. Colonel Butler recklessly rushed up and down in front of his men urging them to stand firm. It was useless. The officers on the right knew the day was lost, as they could see the Indians sixty rods in their rear and the awful havoc they were creating. The drummers were ordered to strike up and the officers refused to give the order to retreat. Soon every captain had fallen. The rear of the army broke away, the Indians after them. As they could not go down the valley they moved towards the river, fighting and falling as they went. The main body followed them. The fight continued as they retreated and was fierce and bloody in the extreme. Many escaped toward Monockasy Island.   The flight across the lower flats made that place the scene of an appalling horror. Nearly two hundred men fled down the valley. The rank grass was stained with blood and many fell and were scalped. The men that reached the river plunged in, some of them to be shot from the shore.

This part of our history is not clear. We learn that Colonel Butler and seventeen men escaped to the mountains, that fourteen men were taken prisoners by the Indians to be the victims of the bloody Queen in the evening. Where were the rest? The next day we find Colonel Denison surrendering the fort to John Butler. Then we have all the rest left to our disposal. Just what hapened the main force after they began the retreat we can only imagine, as they were behind the Indians, they could escape. We are told they fled instead of wisely surrendering to the Canadians. Out of 300, some authorities say, only 165 were found to be killed or missing. We have the impression in reading the account of the flight across the lower flats to the river that the whole force was flying with the Indians after them and striking the most of them down. This was **not so.** We also read that with the one hundred women and children fleeing over the mountain there was only a few old men. During all the journey through the swamp, there is no indication that any of the nearly two hundred men who had escaped had joined them. Where were they?

The upper and lower flats are strewn with dead, and dead bodies are floating down the river in sight of the people on the bank.

Men hid under the bushes in the water; some swam down the river with bullets striking around them, others crawled under rocks and in hollow logs, some ran as long as their legs would carry them. They went across the mountains, down the valley, anywhere to escape. They were desperately frightened, as well they might be, for all who did not speedily put themselves out of reach of the Indians' spears, tomahawks, and scalping knives, were murdered without mercy. The individual tragedies on the river and island were as fearful as those on the plain, while those taken prisoners had to face and suffer a fiendish death.

The picture we have of the scene at Wyoming in the evening epitomizes the manner in which the Indian gratified his revenge and hatred of the white man. It may be exaggerated, but it is quite probable that it fails to convey to our mind an adequate conception of what occurred. The numerous assaults that were made upon the scattered homes of the valley and in other sections, were as fearful and similar only on a smaller scale. We refuse to turn this picture with its face to the wall. It is indelibly engraven on the minds of the civilized world and will remain.

The Indians planned to celebrate the victory they had won. Not a victory for the British, but for themselves. They had more scores to settle than their white friends. They always celebrated their victories with a dance, when they tormented and tortured their victims. This was a natural way, all humanity having the same instinct and a proclivity to do it in the same manner.

A fire was built on the level plain. The prisoners were brought within the center, where they could witness the delight and feel the hatred of their tormentors. They knew how to get up a dramatic scene of the most fearful and spectacular character. The one at Wyoming was complete in every particular. The Indian was dressed for the occasion. The scalps were gloated over. They struck up their awful music and performed their grotesque dance. They shouted, whooped and grinned, the scene becoming a wild carnival that filled the hearts of the savages with delight. They knew that on the morrow they could turn themselves loose and plunder and burn without restraint. They come to the valley for revenge and plunder, and their day had come. They were wild men and this was their reward. Let us pass over the fate of the victims that suffered and were left mutilated and lifeless when the orgie was over. Queen Esther had presided and the death maul had done its work. The men who escaped at that time give us a good description that leaves little for the imagination.

The man that was held in abhorance and designated by the settlers a Tory, was sipping the honey of revenge. No words can describe how he was hated, and history does not give us a record of what he suffered or of the wrongs he endured. This valley was not a paradise for him. He was an enemy, an enemy that had no place to live unmolested unless he left this region. He was often helped to leave, and the hands that helped him are liable to handle him roughly. It is said that seventy of them were in the center of Capt. John Butler's line of battle. There is every reason to believe that those who had gone to Canada instigated the invasion and that those at Tioga joined the company and came back to see and help annihilate their enemy. They thought after the fight pleasant thoughts and planned to return, with interest, all that the settlers had coming to them. Everybody at the upper end of the valley were overjoyed except the men hiding in the forest.

CHAPTER V.

WHEN THE SHADES of evening fell the old repose rested over the plain. The longest day will pass and become only a memory. There could be no repose for the people at the fort. The Indians do not leave their victims to suffer or to survive to drag out a miserable existence. The men stretched out on the flats were sleeping secure from the ills of life. At the fort there was no rest. In the evening Capt. John Franklin arrived with a company of thirty men from Salem and Huntington. Men had escaped from the fight with fearful tidings of the conflict. These had eager listeners to their tale of woe. The women must be protected, they proposed to defend themselves. This conclusion was as impracticable as their plan to bring the cannon from Wilkes-Barre. It might have made a noise, but as they had no ball for it, it could not serve any other purpose.

Every woman was wondering if her husband, son, brother or father was alive or dead. No one could know whether they had occasion to weep or rejoice. After all they had passed through, this night must have dragged its length intermainably long, as they bitterly thought of the morrow. Evil news has swift wings, for when the morning began to cast a glow in the east men who had come in and reported that the people who were not in the fort were getting out of the valley as fast as possible, down the river and across the mountain. The next thing before them was to wait for John Butler and put up with what followed.

John Butler and Colonel Denison met that morning in the Myers homestead, near the fort, and agreed upon the terms of surrender. Life and property were to be respected and the Tories were to be allowed to return and peacebly occupy their land. John Butler was a portly, good-natured man about forty-five. He admitted that he could not restrain the Indians from burning and plundering. The Indians began at once to show their independence of authority by helping themselves to everything they wanted and even commanding Colonel Denison to part with some of his belongings, which they coveted. Nearly every home became a torch. We will refer to an account, written in 1828, by Col. John Franklin, and published in the Towanda *Republican*.

This writer informs us that all the able-bodied men were not at Valley Forge with Washington, and that all the women and children went over the mountain through the shades of death. The awful pall that we find enshrouding all the other accounts is missing, for we feel the presence of live, vigorous men. Our histories are so melancholy that when we read them an old ghost moons about in our imagination like a lost soul in nowhere land. Colonel Franklin's account of the reasons why the men met the enemy makes it evident that it was feared that the invaders would burn the homes and drive off the stock and leave the valley without any opposition. The version he gives of the Queen Esther episode is irreconcilable with the standard story. He says a body of men, numbering fifteen or twenty, had rushed into the river after the fight. The Indians and Tories appeared on the bank and promised that if they would return they would not be harmed. They swam back. They were placed in a circle with an Indian behind each man, then Queen Esther went around the circle with an Indian death maul and brained them all except one or two men, who broke away and escaped. He repeats the assertion that the opposing force outnumbered our men more than two to one, that there were 700 Indians, 400 Canadian troops and 70 Tories, yet it is more than likely that John Butler's official report was correct, in which he states that his force all told did not number over five hundred men. Colonel Franklin tells that a large number of the soldiers surrendered on the battle field and were afterwards inhumanly murdered. When he states that Col. John Butler did not stay long at Forty Fort, but crossed over the river with his men, went down to Wilkes-Barre, and in a few days left to draw the savages out of the valley, as they were burning up the homes in every direction, as well as driving off the cattle, it is evident he knew personally some facts in his statement.

The well-worn road leading from the valley to Strouds-burg, a distance of seventy miles, at that time led through a dense forest and dangerous swamps, very appropriately called the "Shades of Death." This was the highway to the east. After the disaster at Abram's Plain, the women and children began their long and toilsome journey over this road for home. They may have all gone together or they may have gone in separate companies. In all the forts there were men and women with a guard of some kind. All may not have sought refuge or went far away at the time of the exodus. The large number of men that escaped from the field undoubtedly hunted up their families as soon as possible.

The picture we have of the flight is one that represents the limit of human suffering and fortitude. If the victims were not women and children we could appropriately call it hades. The hardships of frontier life had hardened them, otherwise they could not have accomplished the journey and endured the hardships. They had left all they had behind them, yet they were of that race that nothing daunts, that nothing can subdue.

The old pewter dishes were buried by the people before they left their homes, and other objects of value. This indicates that they expected to return. When the exiles reached New England, most of them hired out until they could return. They were real aristocrats maintaining themselves by their own exertion, and fighting their own battles. As the long procession winds its way through the gloomy forest, we like to think them cheerful, and that they sympathized with each other. They were neighbors and friends. These things went a long way and helped to keep their courage up.

The environments and the circumstances are so unfamiliar to us as to make it impossible for us to picture the pathetic incidents of the journey. A mother carrying her dead child for miles, births and deaths under the circumstances, and the hardships of the forced march are things that appear to us only indistinct and blotted pictures.

Spaulding and his men turned about when news reached them of the defeat of their neighbors, and Franklin returned to his home. The dead lay where they fell, wet by the dew, and fanned by the breeze, until September. The summer days went by without a thought of what was taking place or of the bloody tragedy of the near past. John Butler went back north to wear the laurels he had won, the Tories to hug themselves for joy as they thought how secure they were in the advantage they had gained. Alas, they did not know the stony and thorny path they had traveled would be a flower-strewn way in comparison to the path before them. The Indian strutted before the admiring squaws as he exhibited the scalps he had taken and the goods he had brought back. He probably had not heard the name of Sullivan. He would hear and feel him in the future. Their beautiful villages would be wiped out. They would be hunted out of the country and in a few years take up their long journey towards the setting sun. The men who had fled in every direction on the fatal day were rounding themselves up; they were hunting up their families and planning to come back and come to stay. Those who stick, win.

The crops are growing without their care-takers to cultivate or gather them; the rabbit plays around the charred remains of the homes and the summer breezes carry the sweet odors across the man-deserted fields.

We think about the poor frightened people out in the wilderness—visions of the mother, gathering her brood about her in the lonely forest at night, trying to bind up their sore feet, quiet their fears and make them comfortable as they stretch out their tired bodies to sleep. How fearfully tired they must have been. It is a satisfaction to think of them out of reach of the enemy they held in unspeakable dread.

It is quiet in the valley now. Here and there a stray animal is wandering about unheeded, or a rooster crowing on a shed and wondering what is the matter. A strange land was this, the Indians gone, and the white man vanished. No wonder that a masterless hound howls in his lonliness with something akin to a human voice wailing in dispair.

Never mind mother, never mind little one without enough to eat, you will come back over this road some sweet day. You, mother, will watch your children play about your house in the beautiful valley, for the Father of us all has you in the hollow of his hand and is working out human destiny for the highest ends. The bleaching bones will be gathered up and decently buried before the snow falls. In the future many will honor their memory and pity the sufferers. The hidden lives you lead and your sad story will be told and a wreath of immortals will be woven for you.

Evening has fallen over the fields. The evening star shines bright and beautiful over Ross Hill, the moon is rising over the Pocono. Lovely night you hide from our sight the cruelty of man to man.

Queen Esther.

CHAPTER VI.

A NUMBER OF the old settlers had experiences as interesting and as unusual as any we find in the novels that captivated us when we reveled in tales of adventures and stories reeking with blood. There are a great many such tales historically true in which members of old families were the actors.

The incident known as Inman's nap has two or more versions. The most popular one is the following: "Richard Inman started with the Hanover company up the valley the day of the battle. At every house they stopped they imbibed liquid refreshments. Inman filled a bottle so that he could have something between visits. The old man could not carry his load, so he lay down. The battle was fought and lost and men were getting out of harm's way. Lazarus Butler was urging his horse along when he came upon Rufus Bennet, who was pursued by an Indian. Bennet caught on to the tail of the Colonel's horse, and away they went. The fleet footed savage had nearly overtaken them when Bennet saw Inman sitting up, rubbing his eyes. 'Shoot that Indian!' Bennet cried. The old hunter swung his rifle to his shoulder without getting up and dropped the Indian as quick as he had often shot a deer on the run.

Four of Richard Inman's brothers were in the battle; two were killed. One swam the river in his flight, and being overheated, died. Two much whiskey probably saved the life of Richard as well as that of Rufus Bennet. Another brother the next winter thought he heard the call of a wild turkey. He took his gun and went after it. The next spring his body was found scalped by the Indians that had deceived him. The Inmans became known as Indian killers and squared up with them with interest. One of the Inmans had notches in the stock of his rifle to tally the number he killed.

Roswell Franklin hated the Indians and was feared and hated by them. First they came and carried away his son and a nephew, after destroying his crops. A year later, when he was away, they came and carried away his wife and four children and went up the river with them. Franklin hurried up from Hanover to Wilkes-Barre, secured the assistance of eight men, and cut across the mountains and came to their route in advance of the party. They hid and waited. A fierce fight followed. The wife and the children lay flat on the ground and the fighting was done over their heads. Mrs. Franklin raised up and was shot. Finally the children got up and ran to the rescuing party. Most of the Indians were killed. History speaks of "Franklin's oath," for he swore vengeance upon his enemies then and there.

Mrs. Zebulan Marcy started across the mountains with the refugees with a babe six weeks old in her arms, and a little child just able to walk, that she led. The infant died on the way. One account says she covered it with leaves and left it, and another account that she carried it many miles to the first settlement, near Stroudsburg, where the people did everything they could to provide for their comfort.

It is interesting to note the fact that a colored man by the name of Gerson Prince fell at the battle of Wyoming. He was born in slavery and had served as servant of an officer. We are not to forget that this section was at one time more intensely slave territory than Virginia.

The story of Stephen Abbott is typical of very many others. He had nine small children. He went to the battle and escaped, taking his family down the river, as many of the men who escaped did. Later on he came back to see if he could secure any of his harvest. While getting his grain in, with the assistance of another man, they were ambushed and killed.

Mrs. Abbott went back east, traveling the nearly three hundred miles depending on the exhausted charity of the people along the way. When the children grew up they returned and claimed the patrimonial land at Mill Creek. The mother also lived to return. Many of the settlers secured more or less of their crops.

Samuel Carey was captured after the battle by some Indians under a chief known as Capt. Roland Monture. He was taken to Fort Mintermute where a young Indian, who was mortally wounded, was dying. Young Carey was given an Indian name, painted and dressed as a savage, taken to the Indian country and adopted by the family. They tried to make the stranger take the place of their dead son, and found little consolation for their loss in that way. There was often a lack of food and much suffering from the cold. Two

years later Carey returned home, as peace had been declared.
The Indians carried many captives from here to Niagara,
as they could find a market for them there.

The story of Frances Slocum is unmatched in history in
a few particulars. It might be called classic. This wonderful little story of a life throws a false glamor over the
Indian and blinds us to the real misfortune of this white
woman who became an Indian in every particular except in
race. Her neatness and cleanliness, we claim, indicated her
origin, yet the Indian is very neat in all that he fashions
for personal adornment. We have a picture of the Indians,
the morning after the battle, at Fort Wintermute, scraping
the scalps they had taken and stretching then on hoops.
Little Frances was taken the second of November, the massacre having occurred in July. As there were only twenty-
three houses in the town before the Indians burned all but
three, the Slocums had but few neighbors. The people were
coming back from every direction and depended upon the
forts for shelter and protection. John Slocum's house, we
gather, had stood the storm. As the Indians had considered
him their friend, they had promised him protection. He
was a member of the Society of Friends. When they learned
that one of his sons was in the battle and was killed, and
that he had taken in the family of a neighbor that fell in the
fight, they regarded him as a traitor. A month after they
had taken the daughter, they returned and killed him. Mr.
Slocum was absent when the visitors came. On the porch
they killed the boy that was staying there. Then they entered without knocking, for even a friendly Indian walks in

unannounced. They took into custody a young son who was lame, then they picked up the pretty little red-headed Frances and stalked out. They also took a little colored boy. We have the scene of the mother pleading for her child as the little one reaches back for her mother to take her. The curtain drops for sixty years. The father and mother are long since dead. The scrap in a paper sent by a trader is read by relatives in Wilkes-Barre, and they go out to Indiana. The Indian village they come to is not a cluster of teppes, the houses are log, and the Indians living quite like white people, and associating with them. Frances is an old squaw, her family married, one of her daughters the wife of a protestant preacher. Civilization had come her way too late. All they found different than in any other squaw were the family features and a few recollections of her childhood. The old woman wisely said no to all their entreaties, saying "I am an old tree and cannot be transplanted." They brought an artist who painted her picture. She sits dressed Indian-fashion, and makes a very striking picture. It is certain there is no painting in the valley that is more interesting. We are told that she came to the station with her visitors, and while waiting for the train, rolled herself in her blanket, lay down on the platform and went to sleep. It is also told that the chief that stole her made a pet of her on the journey up the river, provided her with Indian playthings and decorated her as he would a favorite daughter. This is the story given by our various writers.

The story of the capture of Frances Slocum, as told by Mrs. Bethia Jenkins, a friend and neighbor of Mrs. Slocum, is as follows, and contributed by Mrs. Mary Reichart of

Florida : "Frances and her mother were standing in a door-way, when an Indian came along with a little boy on his shoulder. The boy was Mrs. Slocum's son (Joseph, I believe), and was lame. Mrs. Slocum pushed Frances behind the door, bidding her to stay there, and accosted the Indian, asking him to give her the boy. 'See, he is lame,' she said, 'he will be of no use to you, give him to me.' This pleading went on for some time, and in the meantime the mother, in her anxiety to rescue her son, quite forgot Frances, who, in childish curiosity, had come from behind the door and stood a little back from beside her mother, and so was un-perceived by her. After a time of parleying with the Indian, he suddenly set the boy down by his mother and in the same moment took Frances upon his shoulder and carried her away. Mrs. Slocum, in realizing this, would weepingly say, 'If only the boy had been taken instead of Frances, how much better I could bear it.' Her thought was that a boy's fate in captivity would be less pitiable than that of a girl."

The adventure of Benjamin Bidlack, another Kingston man, is the first touch of humor in the story of the valley, and this was serious humor. The Bidlacks have left a fine record behind them. To jumble up a foolish song we might say : "They could fight and they could pray, and were the bright-est and best men of their day." Ogden captured Benjamin and made him a prisoner in the fort at Sunbury. Benjamin like Paul and Silas, sang in prison. He sang so well that he was brought out to amuse the officers. They did not know Benjamin or they would not have given him all the room he wanted to act his song of "The Swaggering Man."

The singer swaggered and sang until he had enlarged his circle sufficiently to bring him near the stockade that encircled the yard. Then he shouted, "Here goes the swaggering man." Over the fence he went, leaving a lot of silly looking officers to swear at each other for their stupidity. Very often old ladies in their white caps and old men around the open fire place have told these stories to the rising generation. There is one other story that has all the elements in it that delights the imagination of youth and quickens the pulse of any who have warm blood in their veins. Philip Hunter went hunting with an Indian. He suspected that the Indian was planning to kill him. They agreed to meet at a certain time. Hunter returned to the tree before the time and hung his hat on a stick and put it so it would deceive the Indian. When the savage returned he saw what he supposed the head of his companion, and put a ball through the hat. Hunter stepped out and leveled his rifle at the would-be murderer's breast. The savage threw open his hunting jacket to indicate he was ready to have justice meted out to him.

The following incident is the finest of the lot to the mind of most boys. Several men and a boy were captured and were being taken away. The party encamped for the night, the men were securely bound, the boy was put under the blanket of a chief, and slept by his side unbound., An Indian sat on a log to act as a guard while the rest slept. The boy could see out from under the blanket that the guard was fast asleep; he could hear the rest of the party snoring. The chief's knife was next the boy. This he withdrew cautionsly and cut the cords of the man next to him. This man freed the rest of the prisoners. After they removed the guns from the sides of the Indians, they each stood over an Indian and all at the same time struck an Indian's skull. The Indians that were not killed jumped up, one was shot, the rest ran away. As they ran one of the men threw a tomahawk and buried it in the back of an Indian. Some years afterwards an Indian was seen at a gathering of the whites who had a lame back. He was asked how he hurt his shoulder, and replied that a white man struck him with a tomahawk.

There are enough stories of adventures to make a large book. The men, women and children taken into captivity suffered cold, hunger, as well fatigue of long forced marches. Many of them were sold at Niagara, after suffering the most cruel abuse at the hands of the Tories at that place. Some escaped, having a hard time to get back. Very often they died of exposure or were overtaken and killed.

Artist Shuscell, former president of the Philadelphia Academy of Fine Arts, painted a picture that represents a scene not unusual. A young woman is bound to a tree, the young Indians are shooting arrows to see how close they can come to her without hitting her. A few old squaws are gathered about her, gloating over her sufferings, and the children stare at her with their dark eyes in which there is no pity. The old Indians sit around smoking and the warriors stand watching their victim, pleased with the spectacle. The fire to burn her is already blazing. This burning at the stake was not a mode of torture learned from the whites, we believe it to be an old practice. There are methods of torture the white man could have taught them more horrible. The Indian was an economist, for he endeavored to do as much harm as he could with the least exposure. Consequently he generally waited until the men were out of reach, then he could attack the women and children, knowing in this way he could bring the worst possible suffering to his enemy. There are some things, in their treatment of their captive women, that they were never guilty of, and the Indian deserves credit for this. Old Chief Mintum complained, when he came to Fort Augusta with his children, that the white people debauched them. He was not the only Indian who had reason to complain. The Indian holds the marriage relation sacred, and is not as immoral as a bad white man. The whiskey the white man taught him to drink proved to be as fatal to him as the white man's rifle.

On the road down the valley below our city there is a memorial to mark the spot where the two Jameson brothers and Ash Chapman were attacked by the Indians. They were going from their homes in Hanover township on horseback to Wilkes-Barre. Near the Hanover Green John Jameson was shot, being hit by three balls. Ash Chapman and his horse were both wounded. The horse turned and went home. Chapman died the next day. Benjamin Jameson's horse carried him out of danger. John Jameson had just married Abigal Alden, a descendent of the John Alden who tried to court Priscilla Mullin by proxy away back in the early days. There is a large oil painting in the Historical rooms representing this scene. It was painted by George Porter, artist, preacher, and writer, a man of genius and one of the greatest in the history of this valley.

Within the last few days a monument has been erected to honor the memory of John Abbott and Isaac Williams at Parsons. William Penn Abbott, a decendant, became one of the ablest preachers of the country. We can consider him as one of the greatest men this valley has among those we are to hold in remembrance.

All the forts and other spots where a tragedy took place on the great battle field that covers the entire valley have been marked by monuments erected by Daughters of the American Revolution. There are many old families who need to have some visible evidence placed in view to declare to the world the service they rendered in the past. A building is a valuable memorial, yet the direct memorial should be placed. There is little doubt that in the course of time all those who deserve public and permanent recognition will receive it.

Tradition tells us that Toby's cave, named after an Indian chief of that name, was the refuge of some men fleeing from the Indians. The cave entrance is so small that the defenders could brain any who dared to crawl in.

Campbell's Ledge has a tradition that a horseman named Campbell rode off this high precipice to escape the Indians that were pursuing him. In late years much interest is being manifested toward everything that pertains to the history of this region.

Some have traced the road that General Sullivan cut through the forest. The historical rooms are the repository of many things of interest. This scribe does not know what became of the one cannon that was so much in evidence and boomed out the dreaded summons of the settlers to fly to the forts for protection.

Hardly one of the old log houses is left, and the old flint lock has become scarce. We have many Indian relics, spears, tomahawks, scalping knives and arrow heads, as well as pottery. It may occur to the reader to ask, how could the Indians manage to handle a spear, a rifle and a tomahawk at the same time; they evidently used all these weapons at the battle of Wyoming. The man without a gun may have carried the spear.

The Frenchman would fraternize with the Indians and live among them. The Englishman was more particular about his company. It is evident that many of the Indians became well acquainted with the whites, and there was more or less familiarity of a social character. We recognize the fact that after the battle Indians were a constant menace to every family, and many suffered at their hands. A bounty was put on the scalp of an Indian, and Indian scalps became of commercial value. It is not pleasant to think of our fathers raising hair for a living.

The following was furnished by Mary Culver Evans:

"The true story of James Bird. Before the battle of Lake Erie, James Bird called on a drafted man, and found his wife and children crying around him. Bird told him that he would take his place. He joined the Wyoming volunteers under Captain Thomas. When wounded and ordered by Perry to 'leave the deck,' Bird refused and kept on fighting until victory had been won. For his bravery Bird was honored among the soldiers, which excited the jealousy of a young lieutenant. The war was ended, Perry had gone. Bird was tired of inaction, and he and a young man named Rankin left to join Jackson in New Orleans, they were pursued, brought back, court martialed and sentenced to be shot, the lieutenant doing all he could to hasten on the execution. Parties had gone on horseback to the governor for a reprieve, obtained it, and were riding back, and were within hearing distance, when Bird and Rankin were shot. Hence the song of the late Hon. Charles Miner, 'Spare him; hark! O God! they've shot him,' etc. After their execution the lieutenant was afraid to stay in his room at night for fear of Bird's ghost, and ordered a guard to stay with him. The second night he committed suicide. I have the story from the late James A. Gordon, who visited Lake Erie shortly after the execution, and saw the three graves, those of Bird, Rankin and the lieutenant." In this connection the following verses may be of interest. It is entitled:

THE WYOMING VOLUNTEERS.

BY ALEXANDER LORD, DRUMMER (1815).

'Twas when the flames of cruel war
  Consumed our brethren in the West,
Wyoming felt the cruel scar
  Which long had stung her tender breast.

She cried, "are all our heroes slain?
  Are there none left my heart to cheer?"
Yes, there's a brave, heroic band
  Will be Wyoming Volunteers.

Wyoming shed a gracious smile,
  To find she had true partiot blood,
Who dare brave danger, war and toil,
  Their only aim their country's good.
She gladly sees them gathering 'round
  Their manly *chief, whom they revere,
Saying, "We will surely grant relief
  Or die, Wyoming Volunteers."

Then quick they form their march in line,
  And bend their course o'er Ross' Hill,
In martial splendor, neatly shine,
  And rattling music loud and shrill.
Now view them in the western clime,
  Paraded in the front of war;
Through marshy fens, o'er boisterous lakes,
  Mingling with true Columbian tars.

They drive the savage from his hold,
  And cause proud Albion's host to fear;
Do mighty deeds, with courage bold,
  Like brave Wyoming volunteers.
When they returned to tread the soil
  Of sweet Wyoming, happy rest!
She hailed them with a gracious smile,
  And felt herself supremely blest.

Yet missed she one unhappy youth,
    Though brave as war's hard fate severe,
Ungratefully erased his name
    From the roll of life and the Volunteers.
In desperate strife the foe he faced,
    His dauntless deeds, his name endears;
And never shall his name be 'rased
    From the memory of the Volunteers.
No, never will Bird be forgot,
    By the Drummer of the Volunteers.
                *Capt. Thomas.

Some places of interest in the valley are:

MONOCKONOCK ISLAND.

On the west side of the Susquehanna. It was here
that the Tory John killed his brother, Henry Pencil, who
had fled to this island from the savages. John afterwards
went to Canada, and was killed by wolves. The Indians
said, "He bad man, killed his brother."

TOBY'S EDDY.

Named for an Indian of that name. Toby's Creek
empties into the Susquehanna on the west side. Toby's cave
is in the vicinity. It is a beautiful spot, but by the Delaware,
Lackawanna and Bloomsburg Railroad passing through it,
its old-time beauty was destroyed.

ZINZINDORF HILL.

Lies in Plymouth, opposite the railroad bridge. Count
Zinzendorf was said to be the first white man that entered
the valley. He came as a missionary to the Indians.

THE TWIN ELMS.

On the right-hand side of the road leading from Kingston to Wilkes-Barre, stand these two trees, a landmark of long standing. Now the town of Westmor covers a once farming country.

DIAL ROCK.

Or Campbell's Ledge, just above Pittston, on the east side of the river, is said to have once noted the time of day, when the sun touched the crest it was noon. The Dial Rock Chapter, Daughters of the Revolution, take their name from this rock.

THE UMBRELLA TREE.

On the west side of the Susquehanna river, opposite Wyoming on the mountain, stood a tree high up above all the others, called the Umbrella Tree, on account of its resemblance to that article. It was also called the council tree. It is said it was a spot where the Indians used to meet in their councils. Some supposed that treasure was hidden there, and some persons dug around the roots of the tree until it was killed. Canes were made of it and sold in 1878 at Forty Fort.

QUEEN ESTHER'S ROCK.

This rock is situated at the southeast of the village of Wyoming. Here Queen Esther, with a death maul, dashed out the brains of the prisoners. Most of the rock has been carried away by relic hunters. It is now protected.

CHAPTER VII.

DESTINY, AS well as the men who had deserted this paradise in the wilderness, willed that the descendants of the Pilgrim Fathers should people this valley and make it the Mecca of the oppressed of all lands. Before their harvest had wasted they were back to harvest it. They came in spite of Indian, Tory, Pennamite or the foreign foe. They were built that way and Providence appeared to see to it that the fittest should occupy the land.

The men from this section with the army at the front, who had come within forty miles, and returned when they heard of the defeat that had taken place—these men, and all from here, must have had their patriotism put to the supreme test. They probably found the suspense they endured, as they were thinking of their families suffering hunger and hardships of every description, more than the danger and the privations they were facing. Postage at that time was often a serious affair to those who were destitute, consequently many found it difficult to communicate a message to their friends.

There are so many extravagant stories told of the wreck and ruin left in the trail of the Indians as they overran the valley that we cannot tell just what to believe. One writer states that there were one thousand homes burned and all the grain destroyed; that one thousand men had gone from here to fight with the Continental army. Accepting Charles Miner's statement, that the population was less than three

The Lost Sister of Wyoming.

thousand before the battle, and the facts we have of the figures given as to the number of men who were in the different companies, as well as the knowledge that men came back early in the fall and gathered grain that they found uninjured, we think the statements unreliable. Many titles to property were burned. This, it is apparent, did not prove as serious as it might at this time. The title that possession and the ability to defend themselves gave, appears to have served them better than any other claim. They must maintain by force against the other claimant until it was possible to secure a title for their land that would be valid.

This valley north, south and west was fringed with settlements that suffered little from the invasion of John Butler. The low lands were filled with malaria, which caused many to go up or down the river or over the western mountain.

Captain Spaulding evidently came to the valley within a few weeks after the expulsion. The men under his command were settlers. It was military occupation, at least, they occupied the forts or a fort. They did not bury the men that were left at Wyoming. The people began to come back from every direction and were to suffer to the limit of human endurance from the state authorities, the Indians and the gaunt wolf of hunger. From this time on for many years there is no correct census of the people handed down to us.

Although the outlook was dark, the clouds were beginning to lift. They could hang out that flag of freedom and no one would pull it down. The standard of St. George had disappeared forever from this valley. No more foreign taxation would be levied and no hand could hinder them from manufacturing what they willed. The long years of the Revolution were drawing to a close so that men might devote their energies at home and look after their own interest. The Indians would be soon forced to start on their long journey to the west, and to extinction as well. The Tory would drink his cup of gall to the last bitter dregs. He found that a traitor was despised the world over. No one wanted him. Many went to England to be rewarded for their loyalty. Royalty raised its chin and gave them a good view of its back.

Before we refer to the two expeditions sent to annihilate the Indian, some facts in reference to the rendezvous of the Indians will be in order. Early in the eighteenth century the Five Nations formed their league, after which they included the Indians of North Carolina and became the Six Nations. Parts of the Delawares occupied the two branches of the Susquehanna under various names. The Moravian missionaries labored among them, there were powerful revivals of religion, and many converts. The missionaries were considered friends of the red men. It has been proven that all the characteristics common to humanity can be ascribed to them; that when they were enlightened and Christianized they are humane, sensible and reliable. In 1802 they removed to Oneida Lake. In 1824 they went to Fox River. In 1830 the Oneidas sold much of their land to the state. There is an interesting description given us of the final departure of the Delawares for their new home. With the sick, infirm and the children, with their relics and scanty furniture loaded on wagons, the strong going on foot, they were accompanied by the music of violins and their mournful chanting. The missionaries began their work in 1740 in New York. They were so persecuted by the whites that they were obliged to remove to Bethlehem. Later they built their town called "The Tents of Grace" at Mahomeny Creek, on the Lehigh River. Later on the whites became so merciless that they removed to what is now Wyalusing, and built a town of forty log houses with an Indian name meaning the "Tents of Peace." They built a chapel and cultivated 280 acres of land. Great numbers were added to them and they prospered until the whites introduced rum. After seven years the Iroquois were prevailed upon to sell all their land east of Ohio. They left their beautiful village on the Susquehanna and started on their long journey, two hundred and fifty in number. Near Tioga Point Queen Esther had her village, composed of some seventy rude houses. The history of that section claims that on the testimony of an aunt of the Durkees, Queen Esther led the Indians at Wyoming, presided at the tragedy at the rock and slew twelve or more prisoners, to avenge, it is supposed, the death of her son. The account states that most of the men tried and a few succeeded in escaping. George Gore was overtaken and murdered. After the horrors of Wyoming Washington sent two expeditions to the Indian country. The First was under Colonel Hartley in September. Captain Spaulding was with him. Butler with his Royal Greens had just fled from Tioga. Colonel Hartley, after burning Queen Esther's town and palace, as well as the other towns in his way, returned to Sunbury. He secured a large amount of stock taken from the valley.

Queen Esther is supposed to have derived her Jewish name from the missionaries. This full-blooded Indian squaw, who has gained more fame than any woman of her race, is often confounded with the wife of a Senaca chief, Catharine Montour, the daughter of a governor of Canada.

The second expedition to the Indian country was occasioned by the indignation of the American people. Congress took action and Washington placed three thousand five hunded men under the command of General Sullivan. He was to remove from Wyoming to Tioga and be joined by James Clinton with two thousand men. They were ordered to treat the Indians with great severity. This force was nearly one-third of Washington's army. They began to move to the north where Butler, Johnson and Brant were prepared to meet them. There were two battles, one at Chemung and the other was at Baldwin. The enemy was defeated, many of them killed, their villages destroyed and their fruit trees cut down, as well as their crops being destroyed. The army returned to Tioga and in a few days began their march to the heart of the Indian country. Some years ago the writer visited the home of the Six Nations. It appears as if nature had planned this place for an Indian paradise, and created the Indian to enjoy it. The expedition was successful, the Indians were driven out and everything belonging to them destroyed. This expedition was one of the most important and successful of the Revolution. It occupied less than two months and the loss of men was less than forty.

It is the last straw that breaks the camel's back. What was laid upon the backs of the people of the valley when they came back was more than a straw, yet it did not break their backs. War is inspiring and respectable. A fight for property between relatives and neighbors is the meanest thing in the world. The cruelties and atrocities afflicted by the savage are tame in comparison. The Pennamites came back under Patterson, and marks the beginning of the second Pennamite war. The Friends possessed the thrifty metropolis of Philadelphia and the surrounding country. The Germans settled from the Delaware to the Susquehanna. The Scotch-Irish on the Juniata and in the Cumberland Valley. There were a few settlers up the West Branch. The Yankee settled the North Branch of the Susquehanna. The rest of the state was an unbroken wilderness. The population of the state was 300,000. The Yankees numbered about 6,000, and were scattered from Berwick to Tioga Point. This was in 1783.

In 1776 the town of Westmorland was erected into the county of Westmorland belonging to Connecticut.

After the Yankees had gained possession of the territory in 1775, Congress prevailed upon all parties to drop the controversy. After the surrender of Cornwallis at Yorktown, and peace was declared, the state petitioned Congress to appoint a commission to dispose of the dispute over the land. Congress did this and Connecticut asked for delay. This was refused, and the commission selected from the different states, met at Trenton the 12th day of November, 1778. The court was in judicial session forty-one days.

The decision was that the State of Connecticut has no right to the land in controversy. This decision did not effect the individual claims of those who had bought their property of the Susquehanna Company. This fact was not made known until long afterwards. After the decree of Trenton Zebulon Butler presented a petition, for the people, to Congress, asking that a commission be appointed to determine their rights. This was not granted.

The new constitution was adopted and the federal court succeeded to all the jurisdiction vested in the special court of commissioners. It is conceded that Connecticut wanted concession of western lands, and to secure them made concessions to the rival claimants. The people in the valley had the state troops straddled on them. They robbed, outraged the women, and acted more hellish than the Indians ever had. The people were poor and lived in huts. They were trying to raise crops and to provide themselves with clothes.

A petition was presented to the Assembly of Pennsylvania for a righting of the wrongs they were enduring and for the appointment of a commission. This was granted. The commission of land-owners were appointed with Alexander Patterson as chairman. They came and virtually decided that the settlers could have one year to dispose of their huts and then get out. The commission divided Wyoming in three townships, the new ones being Stokes and Shawanese. Justices of the peace were elected and the Yankees were not permitted to have anything to say in the elections. The commission reported that the settlers holding land under the Connecticut title before the decree of Trenton would receive compensation for their land provided they delivered up possession before April the first, 1783, that is, the next spring. This meant expulsion. Patterson returned with two companies of state troops, assumed full authority, and changed the name of Wilkes-Barre to Londonbarry. Col. Zebulon Butler protested against the lewdness and licensiousness of the soldiers. He was arrested for treason with several prominent citizens of Plymouth, taken to Sunbury, put in a loathsome prison, starved and insulted. Patterson's tenants were put on their property and their stock driven off. The people had their barns burned, their cattle seized, and their wives and daughters the victims of the licentiousness of the soldiers. Patterson was bent upon driving the settlers out. Mock trials were held and decisions were given that became unbearable. They resisted. Patterson made this an excuse for the last act of cruelty in the calendar of crime. One hundred and fifty families were stripped of all they possessed and once more driven from the valley. They went by the way of the Lackawanna, sixty miles to the Delaware. This was the flight through the Shades of Death.

Modern theology is elminating hell. We all hope there is one and that Patterson and his ilk are in it, whatever happens to us.

Patterson seized the property and a great flood in March obliterated all the boundary lines.

The news of this outrage flew over the land and the people were indignant, nowhere more than in this state. The state troops were ordered to disband. The sheriff of North-

umberland, then included in Wyoming, was sent to restore
order. The fugitives were sent for. Patterson was mad
clear through and went in defense at Forty Fort, and prepared for war. Two young men, named Elisha Garrett
and Chester Pierce had been slain by Patterson while gathering in grain. Now the settlers proposed to hunt Patterson
and the Pennamites he had put in possession of their land.
John Franklin organized all the men he could find. He
swept down the west side and up the east, and the Pennamites were routed out. Then he attacked the fort and was
repulsed. Civil war now openly prevailed. Forty of the
settlers were indicted and taken to Sunbury. Then the authorities of the state sent officers to dispossess both sides,
and demanded the arrest of all. Then four hundred militia
came from Northampton county, and by treachery they secured sixty-eight of the setlers, bound them and carried them
to jail at Easton and Sunbury. The next difficulty was to
get rid of the women and children.

At this point Colonel Armstrong was confronted with
the censure of the state authorities. A counsel of censure
was appointed, which reported that the settlers had been
greatly wronged.

The executive counsel paid no attention to the decision
and Armstrong came here with one hundred men and attacked the settlers without success. William Jackson was
wounded. Franklin seized the rifle, covered with the blood
of the wounded man, and holding it up swore that he would
never lay down his arms until death arrested his hand or
Patterson and Armstrong be expelled from the valley, and
the people be restored to their rightful possessions.

General Armstrong began an attack upon the homes of the people. This led up to the passage of an Act of Assembly that gave the people in the valley some assurance of peaceable possesion of the land.

Patterson and Armstrong were recalled, and this ended the second Pennamite war in 1784. The agony was over. The people were in a desperate state of poverty. Winter was coming, they had no harvest to gather and no houses to shelter them.

The last Pennsylvania claimant to leave the valley was Squire Mead. One morning he found the Yankees mowing his meadow. They told him, "It is you or us; we give you fair notice to quit, and that shortly." This was virtually a declaration of war against Pennsylvania. The authorities of this state took the hint. A general pardon for offenders was offered, the law dividing the townships was annulled and all the people were required to swear to keep the peace. They did not comply and that part of the law fell dead.

The people, while nominally under the laws of the state, virtually governed themselves.

On September the 25, 1786, the county of Luzerne was erected. It gave them representation in the council and the Assembly.

CHAPTER VIII.

EN BECAME tired and disgusted with trying to establish titles to the soil by force. It had taken them a long time to realize how futile it was to ravish the land, shut up good men in foul prisons for nothing and burn the homes over the heads of helpless women and children. When they were ready to let the courts settle their disputes a new danger appeared. Connecticut being suspicious of any settlement made by the state authorities conceived the idea of forming a new division, that is, cut off from the state that portion and form a body politic independent of Pennsylvania. This scheme split the people in two. The wise heads were as suspicious of Connecticut as Connecticut was of the State of Pennsylvania. The new plan made a great stage play for a time. The Green Mountain Boys with Ethen Allen, came to the valley. Half-share rights were issued in great numbers and strangers flocked here. Ethen Allen arrested John Franklin and a very unpleasant chapter of our history was endured.

This trouble proved a blessing, as the governing authorities were obliged to step in, and in disposing of the ambitious Connecticut schemes, the titles over which blood was shed were settled for all time.

In 1787 the Confirming Act was passed. This act conceded the land to the Connecticut settlers. The Pennsylvania claimants were to be justly compensated.

When the state authorities began to be just and generous they did not stop at their first act. In 1790 they repealed the act that obliged the occupants of the valley to make any compensation to holders of the charter that a king had given William Penn to liquidate a gambling debt that the sovereign owed young William's father. When the controversy ended most of their troubles were over. Washington was in his grave and the government was steering out into the open sea. Napoleon was at the top of his unparalleled career and the Goddess of Liberty smiled upon a free people. There are many things of interest to consider at this time before we stop to inquire the meaning of military activity among the citizens of the little sleepy town of Wilkes-Barre and in the neighboring villages. The fighting was not all done yet, as elsewhere the trade of war was carried on.

By this time the Indian trails over which the advance guards had pushed their way had become the highway of civilized man. Matthias Hollenback had furnished the people with about everything they could not provide themselves with. The hunter began to till the soil and the people began to be self-dependent. To us it appears wrong that they should convert most of their corn into whiskey for the market. Whiskey was more than a beverage, it was as good as the coin of the country, for they could transport corn in liquid form to the distant market cheeper than the corn itself. The only thing they could manufacture for the market was whiskey. They must produce something they could sell for cash. Distilling whiskey was an occupation that was a source of wealth to every family able to build a distillery. They called it "liquid sunshine." They made it pure and were able to drink it straight. There were no temperance societies and the pulpit favored it as much as the congregation. Later on the government undertook to tax it and a three months' war followed.

For some reason every movement to provide means for educational purposes by taxation failed and most of the teaching was imparted in paid schools. It must be remembered our fathers believed in education and considered the church and school house indispensable. It is common to consider our coal as a source of wealth of which the settlers were ignorant. This is not true. We find that the Susquehanna Company, in 1763, in granting land reserved the coal. During the Revolution coal was mined and sent to Carlisle for the forges of the United States army. We have indications that coal was used by the people who preceded the Indians. It was not believed, however, that the coal went deeper than a short distance beneath the surface. By 1820 digging coal to be carried down the river in arks became a source of revenue. In 1807 coal was shipped to Havre de Grace and sold for eight and nine dollars per ton. Many experiments were made to burn it in grates, and the people could hardly be persuaded that stone coal could be used as fuel for domestic purposes.

Col. George Shoemaker sent nine wagon loads from Pottsville to Philadelphia. Some he sold and the rest he gave away, and was arrested for swindling the people. The coal was put in a furnace to test it. They blew into it from the open door, but it would not burn. They shut the door in disgust and went to dinner, and when they returned the furnace was red hot. The draught problem was soon solved and coal came into general use. It is quite certain coal was used for domestic purposes from 1803.

The population in 1800 in Wilkes-Barre was probably not more than three hundred. The social life was one of perfect equality. The standard of intelligence was equal to that of New England. Agriculture was the chief employment.

In 1791 our Congress imposed a duty on distilled liquor of four pence per gallon. War followed. The excise officers of the government were arrested and tarred and feathered. After mild measures had failed to enforce the law, Washington, in 1794, raisd an army of 15,000 men. Capt. Samuel Bowman, with the Luzerne Volunteers, joined the main army, which soon struck terror to "Tom the Tinker," as the whiskey boys were called, and the insurrection ended.

In 1799 the French war began. The French were at war with the civilized world and considered they were entitled to some assistance from this country. It was not given and war was declared. Capt. Samuel Bowman, with seventy-five men went to the front. This war cloud faded and then we soon had trouble with England. That country came back for one more kick and was accommodated. In 1813 Capt. Samuel Thomas, at the head of the Wyoming Matross, left Kingston and embarked at Toby's eddy with thirty-one men.

Luzerne furnished other men who volunteered. Recruiting stations and barracks were located in Wilkes-Barre. In 1814, when Baltimore was threatened, Luzerne furnished some companies that did not go farther than Danville, as their services were not needed.

In 1846 the Wyoming Artillerists left for the Mexican war under Capt. E. L. Dana. There was a great celebration when they returned, covered with glory and scars.

At the beginning of the Civil War, the first war meeting was held in Wilkes-Barre in 1861, Hon. H. B. Wright presided. Eight regiments were organized for the three months' service. The 143rd Regiment went out under Col. E. L. Dana. Many men from the valley served in the war. Col. R. Bruce Ricketts performed distinguished service at Gettysburg, and Gen. E. S. Osborne made a record. Camp Luzerne was located back of Luzerne Borough.

We will bid adieu to the call to arms and consider what belongs to our history apart from the outside world.

Some one, with a nice idea of fitness, has called our city a queen and a jewel. We agree, thinking of our wealth and culture. It is, poetically speaking, the hub of the valley, a center where many of our own and other lands find a home, and prosper. One John Durkee was its creator and dedicator, in 1772 It included two hundred acres of land and twenty or thirty houses that we would not use for stabling stock, three forts, and a small population reputed to be our peers. We can measure them by the law they passed that rated idleness the chief crime in their calendar of offences. As the town or village increased in numbers the fathers enlarged their boundaries, this was done several times. They certainly were advocates of peace for the constable appears to have ranked as the most important man among them. March 17, 1806, is next in importance to July 3, 1778, for then they assumed the dignity and the burden of being an incorporated borough. The to-be-great and famous offspring grew in stature and favor. It waded in mud and thrived on malaria and its antidote. The first borough election was held and sixty voters elected Jessie Fell burgess and Messrs. Hollenback, Butler, Wells, Colt, Palmer, Miner and Bowman councilmen. Every absentee of a regular meeting was required to pay a fine of twenty-five cents. As a fact of history it is mentioned that Matthias Hollenback paid the first fine. As he was a millionaire, the man who controlled the trade with Indians and whites from the borough to Niagara, the most Courtly as well as the best dressed gentleman in our early history, no comments are in order. At this time there were some forty-eight houses and five hundred inhabitants. The greatest local event prior to this time was the sojurn of a number of visitors at Arnet's tavern. They were royalty out of a job, but one of them afterwards became king of France. These visitors were here 1797.

Before the borough was created a number of men embarked in the seductive enterprise of building ships on the river bank. They were poor sailors, so they were satisfied after they had come to grief in trying to float their sloop out into the open sea.

Kingston, as it is at the present time, was the Eden where the finest fruits of aristocracy, wealth and culture flourished in perfection. The citizens of Wilkes-Barre could not afford a bridge to get over into the promised land, and as they must needs go over they established a ferry They felt humiliated in going down to Northampton street and being carried over like cattle, so they went down in their pockets and built a bridge at the end of West Market street in 1807, that cost forty thousand dollars. We wonder where they borrowed the money. They were eleven years building it. Nature objected to being spanned. The next year one of the piers refused to shoulder longer the burden put upon it. The state was appealed to for assistance. The bridge, after it was repaired, tried to butt against a hurricane, but the attempt was a failure. Consequently in the winter of 1825 the people had to go over the river on the ice. The state, wishing to help the east-siders over into paradise across the river, furnished more money. This money was only loaned, and our honest and forehanded forefathers repaid it. The debt was twenty-eight thousand dollars. Money was scarce and eggs were more current than coin.

The court house did not cut as much of a figure as the court house bell. The people sent to Philadelphia and had one brought here at considerable expense, a year before the borough was erected. About all public proceedings and private acts were regulated by the ringing of this bell. The court house served every conceivable purpose, and next to the taverns, was the center religiously, politically, officially, criminally and socially.

The Valley from Campbell's Ledge.

The second year after the people had incorporated themselves they made an attempt to form a fire department.
Eight dollars they voted to purchase suitable fire extin-
guishers. They failed to make the purchase. This attempt
to supply the town with a fire engine led to the purchasing
of a patent fire extinguisher in 1808. Every year until 1818
it was voted that a fire engine be purchased, and then the
grand jury helped them out with two hundred dollars for an
engine, and forty dollars for the erection of an engine
house..

Court convened for a time in Kingston, but Wilkes-Barre
wanted it transplanted to their center, and as they had that
wonderful bell, they secured the court of justice, so called.

Before 1800 Wilkes-Barre had two newspapers. Our
first historian, Isaac A. Chapman, being the editor of one of
the early weeklies.

Our city is located on the beautiful strip of land on the
east side of the Susquehanna. This matter is being adjusted
in a natural way. The west side is gradually becoming the
center of wealth, population and industrial activity.

Wilkes-Barre became a city in 1871. We will go about
the old town when nearly all the families were to the manor
born.

Rev. Rufus Lane is preaching in the old church on the
Square. Isaac Osterhout is accumulating the money that
built the library and Historical Society building. Anthony
Brower and Barnet Ulph are familiar figures on the street.

Daniel Collings is postmaster, Jonathan Buckley is the sheriff, George P. Steel is the proprietor of one of the famous hotels. Lord and John Butler have a steam grist mill, Jude Kidder and Lawyer Nicholson have law offices on the Square. Dr. Boyd has his office near by. Up at the corner lives Judge Scott and near by is the tavern of Archippus Parrish, a sort of Westmoreland club-house. A brother of Frances Slocum lived on the south side of the Square. Near by Oliver Helm had a cabinet shop. Samuel Howe had a tin shop near the corner. Conrad Teeter, the old stage driver, lived in Rag Row, where he could hear the ring of the hammer of Mr. Lanning on his anvil. General Isaac Bowman lived on that side of the Square. Up Main street was Buzzard Row, where Alderman Gilbert Burrows had his office. Above this Benjamin Drake had his blacksmith shop. Oliver Hillard and Dr. Jones lived up this way. Up a short distance we find the original Myers, John. The fine residence of Ziba Bennett was on Main street, and just beyond the Square, Lawyer Winchester had his office. Farther up George Dennison, Dr. Jackson, Sharp D. Lewis, Gilbert Barnes and Dr. Thomas Miner lived, and Mr. Gilchrist had his shop. On West Market street we find Ebenezer Bowman, Gilbert Laird, Abram Thomas, Thomas Hutchings, Mrs. Nancy Drake, Jacob Sinton, Sidney Tracy and Col. H. B. Wright. On the corner of Franklin and Market there were some beautiful Lombardy populars. The old jail was on East Market street. Some of the other residents were Geo. M. Hollenback, Orlando Porter, Judge Shoemaker, Andrew T. McClintock, Judge John N. Conyngham, William C. Reynolds. These men lived on

River street. The most famous man in town was a Dutch-man or German, that the people puffed up with praise. He was town janitor, and was known as Old Michael.

Up above Wilkes-Barre we find the Miner, Wilcox, Abbott, Courtright, Blanchard, Parsons, Johnson and the Stark families. The ancestreal estate of the Stark family was at the Plains and, like so many of the old families they came from Connecticut. The first to come here dates back to 1734. Mrs. Elizabeth Stark is his great granddaughter. Like the record of most of the old families the pioneer members served under Washington and suffered and fought in the early days. She married Charles, the son of Jacob Shoemaker. David Scott Stark represents the family at the present time.

It is quite impossible to turn away from our past without mentioning the old familiar names.

Down in old Shawnee there was the bluest blood, real men, noble and true. The old families were the Nesbitt, Smith, Davenport, Wadhams, Gaylord, Van Loon, Turner, Atherton, Reynolds, Fuller, Gabriel, Ransom, Wright Pringle, Harvey, Bangs, Rogers, Shoemaker, Rimus, Shonk, Eno and Garrahan.

The old families of the west side were Gore, Pettebone, Bonham, Mathers, Laphey, Bowman, Hancock, Blakesley, Cramer, Snyder, Carpenter, Holegate Raub, Bennet, Atherton, Shoemaker, Smith, Tuttle, Denison, Buskirk, Tripp, Hunt, Swetland, Bay, Perkins, Breese, Miller, Schofield,

Larnard, Hice, Goodwin, Jenkins, Sharps, LaFrance, Cowder, London, VanScoy, Jones, Jacobs, Polen Carpenter, Capin, Slocum, Lewis, Pettebone, Snowden, Underwood, Myers, Church, Reese, Dorrance, Barkers, Thomas, Strohs and Bryant. These are the families between Goose Island and Abram's Plain, not including Kingston. The families of that town were the Gallup, Curtis, Barnes, Hoyt, Reynolds, Myers, Buckingham, Parker, Loveland, Bidlack, Gates Roberts, Covert, Payne, Skeers, MacFarland, Rice, Jaquish, Keller, Devans, Snyder, Taylor, Butler, Pringle, Owens, Sealey and Belding. This takes in everything to Blindtown and Poke Hollow.

The following families lived in and below Wilkes-Barre, most of them names familiar in the early times. The faces of many members of these families are as familiar to us as the face of the court house clock. The names are Quick, Nagle, Inman, Fisher, Downing, Ruggles, Blodgett, Dilley, Horton, Garringer, Mills, Lee, Maffett, Ross, Cady, Stewart, Dana, Dyer, Covell, Dennis, Perry, Ross, Collins, Wurts, Hakes, Greene, Lynch, Whitney, Howe, Mallery, Dupuy, Morse, Gildersleeve, Cahoon, Davis, Vernett, Laird, Babb, Sturdevant, Horton, Hartzell, Jamison, Learn, Lazarus, Sivley, Spencer, Espy, Thomas, Minnich, Kocher, Hurlburt, Franklin, Pell, Chapman, Pierce, Rummage, Askam, Detrick, Deerhammer, Shoemaker, Fisher, Bennett, Hoover, Marcy, Metcalf, Hyde, Blackman, Shafer, Sorber, Rinehimer, Keithline, Lines, McCarragher, Dow, Young, Kidder, Fredrick, Bergold, Ritter, Brown, Landmesser Pease, Keizer, Cook, Preston, Carey, Knock, Sterling, Bunny.

I have built a bridge to span a hundred years. My former treaties on Wyoming Valley spanned the years of the nineteenth century. During the first years of the twentieth century we have had to fight the savage, the Tories and the enemies of civil liberty over again. Our breakers and culm banks may seem blotches on the landscape. I rather regard them as brooches, pinning our beautiful valley to the blue fringe of the hills, with a diamond luster. We go to the top of Prospect Rock, Campbell's Ledge, Penobscot, Tillbury Knob or Fairview, and find there is enough natural beauty remaining to content us. The song of the prosperous present is just as sweet to our ears as the song of the harvesters and the sad music of the winds in the pines to the former owner of this delightful region. Those who follow in our tracks will not find diamonds under their feet as we find them to-day.

This production is an artist's picture of the past. A picture of the present time would be, if well painted, a magnificent frescoe, representing cosmopolitan life, enjoying a degree of prosperity and opportunity for development such as the masses have never known before. Everything that the world has to offer is here in abundance within the reach of all classes. The poor and ignorant become informed and prosperous, while ability is in demand and compensated. Our life is not spectacular, dramatic or picturesque; it is industrial, domestic and material. Men devote their energies to establish and maintain a home and educate their children, consequently we have a condition that is making the best things in life common property.

The men of the greatest usefulness avoid publicity. The officials of our churches, of the many societies organized for specific ends, such as the Historical Society, the United Charities, the Board of Trade and many other organizations are composed of those who serve the public without reward or comment.

There are seventy-five breakers, more or less, that send a million tons of coal, more or less, each, to the market every year. Four or five great railroads run through our valley, which, with numerous large manufacturing plants, form the foundation or our prosperity.

We have a model modern mayor, and Board of Trade president. Fred. E. Kirkendall, our mayor, like W. L. Raeder, the president of our Board of Trade, is identified with nearly every interest and movement, charitable, social and industrial. Our men of means erect large business blocks, and public institutions, as they are needed and invest capital in industries that are worthy of support.

Our leading merchants are Jonas Long's Sons, The Boston Store, Beneschs, Weitzenkorn, Phelps, Lewis & Bennett, Isaac Long, Joseph Coons, Kaschenbach, Carpenter, Voorhis & Murray, Lazarus, the Globe, Simon Long, Bee Hive, Hance, Walters, Miller and others. J. L. Raeder, Robert Baur & Son and the Yordy Co. have large printing establishments. There are two morning and two evening daily papers of a high order.

Among the many we might mention that are before the public are Lyman Howe, of moving picture fame; Sadie Kaiser, the singer; Daniel L. Hart, dramatist and wit; Arnold Lohman, violinist; Father Murgus, inventor, Wesley E. Woodruff, writer, lecturer and critic, and C. Bow Dougherty, colonel of the 9th Regiment.

Prominent citizens who have died within the last score of years are Nathaniel Rutter, Calvin Parsons, W. W. Loomis, Garrick M. Harding, Charles Miner, R. J. Flick, J. C. Powell, F. B. Hodge, Allan Dickson, C. M. Conyngham, R. C. Shoemaker, Charles Dorrance, Sheldon Reynolds, B. G. Carpenter, C. F. Ingham, W. P. Miner, A. T. McClintock, E. L. Dana, L. D. Shoemaker, E. P. Darling, Vaughn Darling, P. M. Carhart, H. B. Hillman, R. D. Lacoe, Richard Sharpe, Lawrence Myers, W. S. Parson, C. Brahl, George Parrish, G. A. Wells, M. B. Williams, H. H. Wells, Isaac Tripp, John B. Smith, Draper Smith, George Shonk, M. B. Houpt, G. M. Reynolds, J. R. Wright, E. R. Mayor, W. R. Maphet, J. C. Phelps, C. S. Morgan, Isaac Long, E. S. Osborne, T. P. Ryder, Thompson Derr. Frederick B. Myers, Joseph K. Bogert, Jonathan K. Peck, John T. Doyle, E. A. Niven, Alfred Dart.

KINGSTON.—The Wyoming Seminary is located here. It is an old town, the center of the west side, and promises to become a manufacturing center. It is not cosmopolitan in its population as are most of the towns in the valley. It is a school and church town. Rev. F. Von Krug, the pastor of the Presbyterian church, has served that congregation for many years acceptable. The present pastor of the M. E.

Church is Rev. J. W. Nicholson, who is highly esteemed. The other churches are strong and are doing good service. Rev. T. C. Edwards, D. D., is pastor of the First Welsh Congregational Church of Edwardsville. He is one of the best known men of his nationality in this country. The presiding elder of the Wyoming District lives here, Rev. L. C. Murdock. He is one of the ablest ministers in the Conference. W. G. Payne and T. L. Newell are successful coal operators; R. P. Brodhead, Charles Laycock, R. B. Howland, D. H. Lake, J. R. Davis, W. N. Multer, N. D. Safford, W. P. Thomas, E. Strouse and many others are active churchmen, and C. O. Thurston, the naturalist, Theron G. Osborne, the poet, and A. D. W. Smith, the geologist, are west side men. The president of the town council, J. W. Marcy, has carried on his wagon business for many years. The burgess of Kingston is C. W. Chapin. W. H. Van Horn is a justice of the peace. Both were formerly business men. C. W. Boughton, tax collector, made wagons for our fathers, and Frank E. Wright has continued the business. Edwards & Co. conduct the largest store in town. A. J. Roat is the oldest and most successful merchant. The old businesses are N. G. Pringle, Dymond & Lewis, James Case, Geo. Carr, Myròn Evans, W. F. Church, C. Bach, Chester Wilcox, Albert Miller, C. W. Turpin and J. A. Burton.

Isaac Jones, the grocer, M. Pooley, Bersch and Frantz have been here nearly as long. Later comers are Cecil Stevens, Millard & Scureman, S. M. Boyd, Doron and Son, and Richard Cronin. Bolton G. Coon and Richard Rosser are successful contractors.

Mill Hollow is where the old mills of the valley were located. As Luzerne, it still follows the old business with many additions, being a more general trading center than the other towns of the west side excepting Plymouth. Dorranceton is the newest and most progressive town of the west side, containing the finest residences and the greatest extent of paved streets. The newly paved roadway between Kingston and Wilkes-Barre was opened to the public on Christmas Day, 1905. Forty Fort is no longer a place of residence only. Large factories are being erected there. Wyoming, formerly Troy, is the location of the monument, a beautiful granite shaft, erected in the middle of the last century to the memory of those who fell in the battle of Wyoming, by their descendants,

East and West Pittston, the latter a beautifully situated residence town, both lying at the head of the valley, form a business and mining center second only to Wilkes-Barre. Plymouth, formerly Shawnee, the home of many of the old families, has at the present time a large foreign population rapidly becoming Americanized. Nanticoke is a city, except in name. Edwardsville is a large and prosperous mining town. Ashley, Miner's Mills, Parsons and Plains are thriving places that should become a part of Greater Wilkes-Barre.

All our cities and towns are growing rapidly in extent and population, and if the wealth accummulating from our present enterprises is devoted to enlarged and diversified industries, the time is not far distant when the entire valley from Nanticoke to Pittston will be one vast and continuous city.

CONCLUSION.

The once familiar things have passed away. The sound of the ax, the crack of the rifle, the hearty laugh, the stage driver's horn and the bob white's whistle. Familiar sights have not even a place in our memory—the old grandmother in the corner, with her pipe, the wood pile, the bars for a front gate, bare feet, the fiddle and the fire place, tallow candles, bare floors and white-washed walls. Every young man does not go to see his sweetheart on Saturday night, and sparking as our fathers practiced is only a legend. There are some things we get on without. Such as shouting in meeting, taking snuff, dancing all night and going home with the girls in the morning. Killing pigs is not the event of the year nor gossiping the chief pastime of the population.

We are not deceived. There is not essentially any difference between us and our forefathers. Of course the dried apples do not hang in strings from our rafters, we do not hold the plow or give quilting parties. We do the same things, it may be, in a less crude way. We worship God, eat the same food, breathe the same air, and look upon the same sights. We are able to provide for ourselves what they had to go without, or have but in part. We, like them, live the old sad, sweet lesson of life, and are thankful that Providence ordained that it should be here in the valley that we love.

HALL OF FAME.

JOHN JENKINS.

Surveyor and prominent man in the early days.

LAZARUS STEWART.

A military hero before the battle of Wyoming.

ZEBULON BUTLER.

Commander of the settlers on the third of July, 1778.

GEORGE DORRANCE.

A soldier of rank and a man of influence in his day.

NATHAN DENISON.

A military leader who surrendered the fort and the men to John Butler after the battle of Wyoming.

JOHN FRANKLIN.

One of the leaders in the conflict with the Pennamites.

GEORGE P. RANSOM.

A hero of the early days with a notable record.

BENJAMIN BIDLACK.

A prominent soldier and citizen.

JOHN DURKEE.

One of the forty settlers and a leader.

ROBERT DURKEE.

Founder and proprietor of Wilkes-Barre.

MATTHIAS HOLLENBACK.

The greatest leader in the industrial life of the valley in our history.

CHARLES MINER.

The greatest historian of our frontier period.

OBEDIAH GORE.

A conspicuous member of a family of early martyrs.

ELISHA HARDING.

One of the first of that notable family to appear in our history.

RICHARD INMAN.

A noted Indian fighter.

THOMAS BENNETT.

One of the members of one of the most prominent families in the early days.

SAMUEL CAREY.

A represntative member of a large and influential family.

WILLIAM ROSS.

Soldier and influential man. Other members of this family appear with an honorable record.

BENJAMIN HARVEY.

Representative member of a notable family.

JACOB JOHNSON.

The writer of the articles of capitulation after the battle of Wyoming.

SIMON SPAULDING.

A military hero of our history.

JAMES WELLS.

One of the early martyrs.

ELISHA SHOEMAKER.

One of the first of that noted family to appear on the pages of our history.

LIBBEN HAMMOND.
A victim of Indian warfare.

ELISHA BLACKMAN.
The father of Major Eleazer Blackman. This family acted a notable part in the early days.

ISAAC TRIPP.
He was painted and killed by the Indians.

JOHN JAMESON.
Victim of the last Indian massacre.

JAMES BIRD.
Shot at Lake Erie for desertion. A brave soldier and martyr.

JACOB CIST.
He was a scientific man, an editor, engineer and one of the most scholarly men in our annals.

JOHN ABBOTT.
A prominent citizen and a victim of the Indians.

JESSE FELL.
The first man in this county to burn anthracite coal in a grate.

WILLIAM HOKER SMITH.
A noted physician and citizen.

FRANCIS SLOCUM.
The lost sister of Wyoming.

ANDREW BEAUMONT.
He filled with distinction positions of great responsibility in the county, state, and nation.

JOHN N. CONYNGHAM.

Was judge of the court of Luzerne county. No man in our history inspired more respect and admiration.

AMZI FULLER.

Prominent man.

GEORGE WOODWARD.

Father of Hon. Stanley Woodward. He was one of the most notable men of the state.

HENRY M. HOYT.

Governor of Pennsylvania. He wrote a valuable work on political economy.

EDMOND L. DANA.

Hero of two wars, jurist and scholar.

THOMAS P. HUNT.

Temperance lecturer, known all over the nation.

WESLEY JOHNSON.

Secured the erection of the Wyoming monument.

HENDRICK B. WRIGHT.

Historian, Congressman and orator.

CHARLES PARRISH.

The greatest captain of industry since Matthias Hollenback.

REUBEN NELSON.

The most noted educator of the valley. The first president of Wyoming Seminary.

GEORGE PECK.

Historian and preacher.

ANDREW T. McCLINTOCK.
Influential citizen.

H. BAKER HILLMAN.
Erected the Harry Hillman Academy.

ISAAC OSTERHOUT.
Founder of the Osterhout Library and the Historical
Society building.

F. B. HODGE.
The honored and loved pastor of the First Presbyterian
Church for thirty-five years.

DANIEL EDWARDS.
The most prominent and successful man in mining coal
in the valley.

EDWARD R. MAYER.
Prominent Physician. Donated the Home for the
Friendless and a large contributor to its support.

JOHN WELLES HOLLENBACK.
Influencial and prominent citizen.

ABRAM NESBITT.
Prominent citizen. Donated Nesbitt Hall to Wyoming
Seminary.

R. BRUCE RICKETTS.
Hero of the battle of Gettysburg.

HENRY W. PALMER.
Congressman and lawyer.

CHARLES D. FOSTER.
Legislator and lawyer.

L. L. SPRAGUE.
    President of Wyoming Seminary since 1882.
HENRY L. JONES.
    Rector of St. Stephen's Church since 1874.
JOHN B. REYNOLDS.
    Builder of the first electric road and the North street
    bridge.
GEORGE B. KULP.
    Author of the Families of Wyoming Valley.

MISS EDITH BROWER.
    Organizer of the Town Improvement Society and writer.

MRS. ROSAMAND L. RHONE.
    Author and artist.

MISS SUSAN E. DICKINSON.
    Talented writer.

FREDRICK C. JOHNSON.
    Historical writer and editor of the "Historical Records."

HORACE E. HAYDEN.
    Historian and secretary of the Historical Society.

OSCAR J. HARVEY.
    Historical writer.

H. B. PLUMB.
    Historian of Hanover Township.

D. L. RHONE.
    Writer on law and political economy.

HARRY A. FULLER.
    Prominent speaker and lawyer.

GEORGE S. BENNETT.

Prominent in finances and church work.

FREDERIC CORSS.

Physician and scientist.

MRS. CAROLINE PETTEBONE.

Donated a gymnasium to Wyoming Seminary. She also left memories that remain like the fragrance of a sweet flower after the blossom has faded.

MISS MARTHA BENNETT.

Erected Bennett Chapel. That was only a small part of what she gave. She had greater gifts than money to bestow.

MRS. H. W. PALMER.

Organizer of the B. I. A. No woman in our history has conferred so much direct benefit.. Few women in the nation have performed so great service for humanity.

MISS HANNAH P. JAMES.

First librarian of the Osterhout Library. No woman has exerted a wider personal influence for the intellectual life of this valley or was held in higher esteem.

MRS. KATHARINE SEARLES McCARTNEY (Mrs. W. H.).

Formed the first Chapter of the Daughters of the American Revolution in the State of Pennsylvania, and the Wyoming Chapter, through whose inspiration all of the forts in this vicinity have been marked.